‖‖‖‖‖‖‖‖‖‖‖‖‖‖‖‖‖‖‖‖‖‖
D0425172

To Lynn —
Stuck with your
dreams (scripts).
        Best

        Ala Nel

Cue the Bunny on the Rainbow

The Television Series

Robert J. Thompson, *Series Editor*

The last shot of the last episode of *The Verdict Is Yours*. Production assistant Meredith Babeaux took it worse than I. *Courtesy of Alan Rafkin.*

Cue the Bunny on the Rainbow

Tales from TV's Most Prolific Sitcom Director

Alan Rafkin

Syracuse University Press

Copyright 1998 © by Syracuse University Press
Syracuse, New York 13244-5160
All Rights Reserved

First Edition 1998
99 00 01 02 03   6 5 4 3 2

All photographs are from the personal collection of Alan Rafkin unless otherwise stated.
Every effort has been made to trace the ownership of all copyrighted picture material.

The paper used in this publication meets the minimum requirements of American
National Standard for Information Sciences—Permanence of Paper for Printed Library
Materials, ANSI Z39.48-1984.∞

Library of Congress Cataloging-in-Publication Data
Rafkin, Alan, 1928–
Cue the bunny on the rainbow : tales from TV's most prolific
sitcom director / Alan Rafkin. — 1st ed.
p.   cm. — (The television series)
Includes index.
ISBN 0-8156-0542-0 (cloth : alk. paper)
1. Rafkin, Alan, 1928–   .   2. Television producers and directors—
United States—Biography.   I. Title.   II. Series.
PN1992.4.R34A3   1998
791.45'0233'092—dc21
[b]   98-20443

Manufactured in the United States of America

This book is dedicated to my daughters, Dru and Leigh.

They have always been supportive and loving and probably the most fun I've ever had. I love them both dearly.

Alan Rafkin is a television director whose career has spanned four decades and more than eighty different television series. He has been nominated for four Emmy awards, and took home the prize for an episode of *One Day at a Time.* He lives in Rancho Mirage, California, and Rollins, Montana. This is his first book.

Contents

Illustrations

Acknowledgments

Thank you to Joseph Schneider, M.D., who has tried his level best to see that I enjoy life, and to Marshall Gelfand, whose friendship and advice have kept me out of trouble for fifty years. Thanks also to Lori Marshall, who took hours and hours of my tape recordings and turned them into a book.

Cue the Bunny on the Rainbow

1.

Upon Facing an Unexpected Retirement

It's June 18, 1996, and I'm scared to death.

I've worked every television season for the past thirty-four years directing sitcoms and I've decided to retire. Well, I don't know whether I've decided to retire or the business has decided to retire me, but I am without a series. I've directed everything from *The Andy Griffith Show* and *M*A*S*H* to *Murphy Brown* and *Coach,* but this season I haven't been offered a show that seems worthwhile. The truth is, I haven't been offered much of anything this year. I'm turning sixty-eight years old next month, and it looks like I'm going to have to get used to a new age and a new job called unemployment.

Some people might say that I'm lucky and that this is a fine time to retire. My business manager and oldest friend Marshall Gelfand has told me that I'm financially secure and I don't have to work. But although the money certainly has had its benefits, I didn't stay in this business for the money. I've raised a family on television. I've never had to take a job outside of the field. I loved the work and that has kept me on the set. And now, when the end of my career is staring me in the face, it's like a reflex. I'm used to sweating out the months between March and June when people scurry around for jobs, and for more than four decades I've never come up empty handed. Until now.

I have two choices: I can retire now and pretend it was my idea. I'm old enough. I don't think anyone would question my motive. Or I can wait around and hope that I'll get offered something mid-season in September or October. That could happen. I've never had to do that be-

1

fore, but maybe it's worth the risk. Then again, what if I get offered nothing? Then I'll have to retire and it will be too late in the season to pretend it was my idea. I'll just look like a dinosaur taking his last few steps through the annals of television. The problem is that I don't feel like a dinosaur.

Retirement is such a frightening and loaded word. It means you don't do for a living what you used to do. I've really only done one thing for a living, and I don't know how to stop doing it. I've been working in television since 1953 when I started as a gofer at CBS, and inside I still feel like I have the energy of that gofer. Despite three divorces, two grown daughters, and three open-heart surgeries, if you put me on a set with a cast and a crew I'll be the first one to crack open the script and get right to work. Television directing is like a drug to me. When I'm on a show I feel higher than any junkie. But when I'm not working sometimes I don't even know who I am. Television has become my passion. My addiction. My identity. I'm a rather short, self-deprecating man who loves to work beyond restraint. If I can't call myself Alan Rafkin, television director, who will I be?

▀ ▄▀ ▄▀ ▄▀ ▄

I am sitting in my boat on the Flathead Lake in Rollins, Montana, where I have built a home. My daughters, Dru and Leigh, are up here visiting me and are reading books and sunning themselves. The only real sign of Hollywood is the name of my boat, *Residuals,* which was christened and paid for by money from some of the situation comedies I've directed over the years. The sky and water are magnificent today, but I can't stop thinking about television. It's when I'm alone in my house or out here in the boat that I start to think about all of the television shows I've been associated with over the years. I've directed more than eighty sitcoms, many multiple times, adding up to some 800 half hours of television.

I've directed some great comedians such as Dick Van Dyke, Don Knotts, and Garry Shandling. I've directed some of television's most talented women, like Mary Tyler Moore, Marlo Thomas, and Candice Bergen. I've directed some actors on their way up including Ron Howard,

Sally Field, and Juliette Lewis, and some actors on their way down like Arthur Godfrey, Robert Mitchum, and Flip Wilson. And now I'm sitting on my boat in Montana about as far away from a Hollywood sound stage as you can get.

My daughters suggested that I write a book about my career in show business. I'm reticent. I'm used to being behind the camera, not center stage. Yet the timing seems perfect. As I am on the verge of self-imposed or mandatory retirement (I still can't decide which), what better time to sit down and write a book? But I don't want to be pompous. I don't want to be precious or saccharine. And I don't want to whine. If I'm going to do it, I want to do it right. I want to tell about the stars that I've worked with, the shows that I've staged, and the fine journey that I've traveled from gofer to prime-time sitcom director.

▅ ▅ ▅ ▅ ▅

Even though I knew from the time I was very young that I wanted to be in show business, that was not an idea that my parents agreed with or even understood. I was born in New York City on July 23, 1928, to Til and Victor Rafkin. They named me Alfred Irwin, a name that I hated and never felt suited me. As an adult, after years of using Alan as an on-screen directing credit, I legally changed my name to Alan. (Oddly enough the day I went to court, Paul Reubens—once known as Pee-Wee Herman—was in the same courtroom changing his name. Years later I would direct him in *Murphy Brown*.) But my name wasn't the only thing I felt uncomfortable about when growing up. My parents thought I was a wise guy and never passed up an opportunity to tell me so. My mother often threatened to pull out my tongue with her bare hands, and I think she probably would have if it had been at all possible.

I was the middle child of three and I spent my early years in the Bronx living in a small apartment along with my sister Claire, four years older, and my brother, David, five years younger. From the time I was about six years old, my father and his brother, Uncle Iz, owned a men's clothing manufacturer called Rafkin Brothers. They did pretty well financially because about the time I was eight, we moved to

Cedarhurst, Long Island, into what I thought at the time was a castle located at 321 Roselle Avenue. I later realized that it was just a small corner house with a little piece of lawn, but when I was a boy I thought it was the Queen's Gardens. It didn't look like anything I had ever seen in the Bronx.

My father was born in the middle of eleven children and he employed many of his relatives, including his unmarried sister Celia, who walked with a limp and served as secretary for my father and his brother. My father used to scream and yell at poor Celia. And he screamed and yelled at my Uncle Iz. And he screamed and yelled at pretty much everybody. To this day, my father is one of the angriest men I've ever met. He seemed to wake up every morning with his fists clenched, ready to fight the world. All of the rage and anxiety he held onto eventually killed him too young with a cerebral hemorrhage at the age of sixty.

When it came to being a parent, my mother didn't have much over my father. When I think of my mother, who died in 1997 at the age of ninety-five, I remember how social she was. Not with me, but with her lady friends. She was one of the great all-time friends to play cards with or go to lunch with. But when it came to showing affection, she balked under the weight of the sentiment. I remember whenever I would hug my mother I could always feel her counting under her breath "one . . . two . . . three . . ." and then she would simply back away and leave me standing alone.

My mother spent her days out of the house with her girlfriends when I was growing up, but even when she was home things weren't much happier. In the evenings she would line my sister, brother, and me up at the front door and we would wait for my father to come home. He would take the Long Island Railroad from his office at 91-93 Fifth Avenue. The minute he opened the door, mother would start in with, "Guess what that one did today? Guess what this one did today?" The child who allegedly caused the trouble was usually me. My father's reaction was to start swinging the *World Telegram and Sun*, which was the newspaper he read. He'd just start smacking anyone who was in his way—again usually me—with the daily headlines.

In the evening, my father would have a shot glass of schnapps, followed by a sip of water, and then dinner would begin. I always ate my meal very quickly (and still do, out of habit) because dinner was often a deadly routine. My parents spoke above us as if we weren't there. Whenever there was something they didn't want us to hear, like the punch line to a joke, they would say it in Yiddish, a language we didn't understand. It was so frustrating, and there was never any typical family dinner-table banter like "How are you?" or "How was school today?" There was either dead silence or the conspiratorial sound of my parents talking to each other. If there happened to be a disagreement at dinner, my brother would immediately push his chair away from the table and run to his room. He just couldn't stand it.

The way I handled the tension was to make my sister laugh, sometimes until milk came out her nose. Then, of course, I would get yelled at by my parents for fooling around. We had an African American housekeeper who was very sullen. But she was a magnificent cook so we ate very well. In fact, we ate so well that I think it saddled me with bad cholesterol for life and led to my heart surgeries. All I ever remember was meat. We ate a lot of meat. We also ate a lot of desserts. Generally we just ate a lot of everything, but it was delicious. But the abundance of food was a poor substitute for the lack of warmth from my parents. Affection was rarely served.

The only thing I can think of in my childhood that may have foreshadowed my career in show business is that I had a sense of humor, much to my parents' chagrin. No matter what was going on around me, I could usually find a way to make it funny for myself, and often for others, too. I remember some of my aunts, amused by a few of my antics, would tell my father that he should send me to a children's professional school to study acting. This would make my father furious. He hated show business and I think secretly he was afraid of it. Everything I found joy in seemed to rub my parents the wrong way.

My unhappiness at home made me search for alternatives. I was intrigued by some kids from our town who went away to high school at Admiral Farragut Naval Academy in Toms River, New Jersey.

They'd come home only on weekends in their uniforms to visit family and friends. Maybe it was the thought of living in another place, or wearing a uniform, or the fact that the parents of these boys were so happy to see them when they came home, but I thought, "That's what I want to do." So, I went away to the Admiral Farragut Naval Academy thinking that it would be the perfect solution to my misery at home.

Unfortunately, it wasn't. On the first day I discovered that part of the drill was to get yelled at by people your own age. I'd gone from living with my parents' yelling to living at Admiral Farragut with more yelling. I called my father and told him I wanted to come home. He said I couldn't go through life starting things without finishing them. I spent the next year and a half at the academy finishing high school.

Whether I was living at home or away at school, my childhood boiled down to being ignored by my parents. I wanted to make them laugh and smile, but they were too busy screaming. I could have handled everything else if I wasn't ignored. Ignored was a big word because shunning was the preferred punishment in our house. To this day I get physically sick if somebody snubs me. You can yell at me, scream at me, or hit me. You can do whatever you want and it won't hurt me and affect me half as bad as if you ignore me. I have always felt out in the cold waiting for someone to notice me. That's just the way things were.

The first time I ever saw a telecast I was in the Boy Scouts. A local drug store had one of the first TV sets in the neighborhood and after a Scout meeting one day a bunch of us went over to watch a basketball game. It was fascinating and mesmerizing to watch the players' images flicker across the screen. Before I knew it, though, time had slipped away and I was late for dinner. When I got home my mother opened the front door and started screaming. She raised her hand to hit me and I raised my hand at the same time to protect my nose, which I had broken ice skating a couple of days before. As our hands collided, she yelled, "Vic, he hit me." My father came downstairs, put me on the floor, put his knee on my chest, and beat the shit out of me. That marked the first day I watched television.

But the rough introduction did not turn me away from the medium. With time we got a TV set in our house and I watched the Friday night fights and several of the variety shows. There wasn't a lot on TV in those days and programs only ran at night, but I remember being instantly attracted to show business. I wanted to be a performer. I don't know if I ever really said it to myself out loud, but in my guts I wanted to be a comedian. I never imagined doing anything else for a living. I never wanted to be a fireman, a doctor, or a policeman. Nothing else interested me. It was my unspoken dream to work in the entertainment industry.

I graduated from Admiral Farragut in 1945 with grades that could only be classified as abominable. With my college choices limited, I ended up at Moravian College and Theological Seminary in Bethlehem, Pennsylvania, after trying to get into Lehigh University, which was located in the same town. An official at Lehigh said that if I went to Moravian for a year or two, then I could transfer to Lehigh. It was a weird experience because Moravian trained young men to become pastors and preachers, and I was one of three Jews in the entire school. I was afraid to make any friends on campus because the entire situation seemed so artificial and temporary. I clearly didn't belong there.

Although I didn't fit in at Moravian, I would be accepted by another group. As a clothing manufacturer, my father used "jobbers," or people out of town, who would do a lot of his work. One of these "jobbers" was a family named Billera. There were seven Billera brothers and they lived in Allentown, Pennsylvania, near Bethlehem. Each of the brothers owned a square city block with a large home and swimming pool. My father said the Billera family would call me at Moravian. One day the dorm phone rang for me and a voice said, "Are you the Rafkin kid? This is Patsy Billera. You're going to come over Sunday for dinner. We'll pick you up."

On Sunday, as promised, a big black Cadillac pulled up with two of the brothers, who looked like clones of Al Capone. Together we drove to the house of Tony, who was the oldest Billera son. We arrived to find the whole family gathered around a huge dining-room table. Wives, husbands, and babies in high chairs circled the table. In the middle of the table was a huge tureen of al dente pasta accompanied by smaller bowls of meat balls, red clams, and white clams. Everything you could imagine. An Italian feast.

I started going to dinner with the family every Sunday night, and I treasured my time with them. It was like going into another world and being welcomed as one of their own. One day Tony Junior called me at school and asked if I would go fishing with him and some friends. I wasn't a fisherman, but I would have gone anyway just for the chance to be with Tony. But I said, for the first time in my life, I had to study. They went fishing without me. On the way, their car went off a mountain road. Tony was killed instantly.

His death was too much for the Billera family to handle. Their Sundays became pilgrimages to the cemetery. The family lost their spark and eventually fell apart. But I will never forget them as the loveliest and happiest family I had ever met. They were so genuinely nice to each other that it almost startled me. I never knew a family could treat each other so well. I never knew people, particularly relatives, could be so good to each other.

◢ ◢ ◢ ◢ ◢

After a year at Moravian, I abandoned my plans to transfer to Lehigh when I was accepted at Syracuse University in 1946. I remember asking my father if I could go and study in the theater department. He said, "Absolutely not. You will be a business major." And that's what I was. I was too afraid to argue with my father. He seemed to know what was best for me, and he wasn't about to let me go against his orders. The only problem was that I had no interest in business. Sitting through my finance classes was the most tedious thing I'd ever done. I tried to make myself pay attention, but I just couldn't tune in.

College wasn't a total loss, however, because I made my life-long friend Marshall Gelfand when I joined a fraternity called Sigma Alpha Mu. Marshall had the interest in business that my father had hoped for me; and today he runs a business management firm called Gelfand,

Rennert, and Feldman with offices and high-profile clients in London and throughout the United States. I'm probably the lowest moneymaker they have as a client, but I get more attention than anybody because I've known Marshall the longest. The solidarity of our relationship has been one of the few constants in my life. Not only has he given me his friendship for fifty years, but his support and financial wisdom as well.

Shortly after my graduation from Syracuse in 1950, I was drafted into the U.S. Army to serve in the Korean War. The morning I left for the service, I remember walking out the front door to find my father sitting behind the wheel of his green Cadillac, warming it up. Usually when we were in the car together he would whistle a random tune or tap his pinkie ring against the steering wheel, anything so he wouldn't have to have a conversation with me. But on the day I left for the army, my father just sat quietly in the car looking ashen. I was going away to war at a time when the Korean conflict was at its height, and my dad was obviously frightened for me. But he couldn't tell me he was afraid. He had to act angry and pissed off, which he became during our car ride. Anger was the emotion he felt most comfortable with. And that still makes me sad because I wish things could have been different between us.

After entering the service, I was sent to Fort Dix near Trenton, New Jersey, for basic training. It proved to be my most meaningful time in the army because at least I knew what the hell I was doing. They trained us until we felt like warriors of strength. A chaplain who had just come back from the front told us that the reason so many young men were dying in Korea was because they were so out of shape. That's all our commanding officer needed to hear. We never walked again. We ran everywhere. We marched until ten o'clock at night. We went to bed and then started it all over again the next morning.

Despite the emphasis on body conditioning, I also learned to smoke in the service. We usually got a break on a march and the sergeant would say, "Smoke if you got 'em." And even though I never smoked before, I'd bum a cigarette and light up. I thought it was an order that needed to be followed. Everything in the army was about orders including the biggest one of all—the day we got the call to head off to Korea. When I called my family to tell them I was leaving for combat, you never heard such crying. Not from them, but from me. I was young, afraid, and didn't know when (or if) I would be coming home again.

Thanks to a strange twist of fate, however, I was never sent to Korea. A few days before I was to be transferred to Fort Ord in northern California in preparation for our voyage to Korea, the first sergeant angrily yelled out my name and six others and told us to report to the orderly room. That night we were put on a train and sent to Fort Meyer in Virginia. Sitting on that train I remember thinking, "Where am I going? And why?" The other six guys were engineers, and I couldn't figure out where I fit in. I had never felt so completely in the dark before. When we arrived I found out that I was there for a Special Services conference, a division of the army that coordinated variety shows and other entertainment for soldiers. I'd been selected to participate because army officials thought I had a background in show business. This wasn't entirely true.

I had exaggerated on my application when I joined the army. They had asked me what I did in civilian life, and I said that I was a theatrical agent. The truth was that I had worked as a secretary for about a month at the William Morris talent agency in New York. The agency taught me enough shorthand and typing to be able to work for an agent named Hal Kemp. The first time he dictated a letter to me, he blew smoke in my face and talked so quickly that I had trouble seeing my shorthand through the clouds of smoke. I tried to keep up with him scribbling longhand, but I just couldn't do it. I quit after a month. So, that's how the army misinterpreted my entertainment experience: I fibbed and they bought it.

While I was stationed at Fort Meyer I also got into trouble over something as silly as my dirty laundry. Fort Meyer was located outside the Pentagon. The day I arrived I was not only wearing dirty fatigues with a two-day growth of beard, but I also carried with me a bag full of dirty laundry. I asked one of the other guys who had been there awhile where the washing machines were. "Oh, it's cool," he said. "You just walk out the barracks, down these subway stairs, and you end up in the mall section of the Pentagon. There's a laundry there."

And so I headed off with my dirty clothes. I thought I was following his directions, but I ended up on the front door of the Pentagon. As

I walked through the door, with my furry face and dirty clothes, a Military Policeman looked at me in amazement.

"Where are you going?" asked the MP.

"To do my laundry," I said.

He arrested me on the spot. I tried desperately to explain my situation, but the MP gave me a citation anyway and then let me go. This was just another example of my unimpressive military career. I rarely got anything right.

I played along with the Special Services unit, however, because I thought anything had to be better and safer than being sent to the front in Korea. The army was looking for people to run service clubs, and one of the interviewers told me about a position available in Alaska. When he started going into detail about transportation by dog sled, I said, "No thank you." I wanted to be stationed closer to home. The closest post I could get was Aberdeen Proving Grounds in Maryland. It was probably available because that's where they blew up bombs.

I was stationed for two years in Maryland where I was the narrator with the second army band. When shows like the Lucky Strike Hit Parade or the Camel Caravan would come to town, I would serve as the master of ceremonies. I slowly started to develop a little comedy routine that I used to introduce the acts. However, even though I was having a good time, I felt a certain amount of guilt in my stomach for a long time. Most of the men who I had sweated and trained with had been shipped off to Korea, and there I was with a microphone in my hand doing jokes. But I was finally working in show business, and I was starting to like it.

While in the Special Services unit, I worked nights and weekends as a disc jockey in a local radio station called WASA in a town called Havre De Grace. I would say, "1330 on your radio dial, the voice of northern Maryland WASA." I pronounced it the smooth French way and was told it was wrong. The station manager, who was always drunk, said, "Jew boy, we pay you to pronounce every God damned syllable. It's Ha-vre-De-Grace." I was instructed to play country western and hillbilly music, which wasn't my kind of music but I played it and said, "Yes, sir." You could tell me anything in the army and I would say, "Yes, sir." Like the old song says, "Keep a smile on your face and your big mouth shut." That was my strategy for two years.

I tried to hide my fear, but keeping all my worries inside began to damage my feet. Yes, my feet of all things. A rash broke out on top of them where the skin is usually smooth and clear. The rash caused my feet to itch so badly that I couldn't stop myself from ripping them open every day and making them bleed. The experience was almost orgasmic. A doctor gave me a note saying that I had to wear white socks, but even that didn't stop the itching.

Finally, I was admitted to Walter Reed Hospital where another doctor examined my feet and said, "This is just a nervous condition related to stress. It will go away when you get out of the service." And I said, "How about I just get out of the service now?" but he wouldn't buy it. They put my feet in casts to try and break the cycle of itching. I then called my parents to let them know I was in the hospital, and also to whine a little about my predicament.

Soon after my phone call home, I was sent into the office of an irate colonel at the hospital, where a member of the American Legion was waiting to meet me. My father had called the American Legion, told them I was being treated badly, and requested that they intervene on my behalf. The truth was that I was receiving wonderful care. My dad had mistaken my whining for a desperate plea for help. I was very embarrassed and assured the American Legion official that I was receiving top-notch care, and sent him on his way. The colonel was not pleased with my blatant waste of his time.

Once I was out of the hospital, I returned to my job at the radio station. One of the announcers I met while working at WASA was a civilian from Baltimore named Ed Bakey, who looked like John Barrymore with his tall, slender build and sharp facial features. More than anyone I had ever met before (even me), Ed loved show business, and the two of us decided to form a comedy act. When USO-type shows would visit

Entertaining the troops, 1951. *Courtesy of Alan Rafkin.*

our base, we would beg the person in charge to let us perform. We called ourselves Bakey and Page. I was Alan Page, which was a name I borrowed from the wife of a soldier who worked at the radio station. I liked the sound of the name.

After serving in the army for two years, I was glad when I was finally discharged. It was not a very popular war, today or even back then. My mother once told me that while I was in the service if one of her friends at the supermarket asked her where I was, she would say, "Oh, out of town." When I was discharged on a Monday early in December 1952, I went to stay with my parents in their new home in Woodmere, Long Island. But I knew I wouldn't be home for long.

Ed and I were supposed to open our act in Harrisburg, Pennsylvania, the following Wednesday. When I told my parents I was going out on the road to perform a comedy act, their reaction was anything but supportive. My father said, "That's very interesting. Could you come into the kitchen? I want to talk to you for a minute." I followed him into the kitchen. As the door closed, he took his right hand and smacked me on the side of the head. Suddenly all of his anxieties for my future poured out. "What do you know about show business? Who do you know who has ever been a success at it? You'll be a failure. You'll be a pimp! You'll be a drug addict!"

My parents thought that anybody who was in show business was either into drugs or prostitution, or both. It wasn't something that I could talk to them about. Their minds were made up and I couldn't do anything to explain away their delusions. So I just left. I have no idea how I scraped up the courage to do such a thing. But I just did it. I packed my bags and headed off to Harrisburg with Ed. I thought, finally, my career as a performer was about to take off.

There was one problem: We bombed. To say that we were overcome with stage fright is an understatement. I had cotton mouth so badly that I almost couldn't speak. We were so nervous that we didn't even give the audience a chance to laugh. We just steamrolled right through our material. Ed was the straight man and I was the comic, but I didn't wait for him to finish a straight line before I came in with the punch line. Looking back on it now, I think that our material was not all that bad. It was our delivery that killed the jokes.

We only performed together that one time, but it was clear that success as a comedy act was not within our grasp. Ed and I remained friends over the years, and I kept in touch with him as he moved to Hollywood where he became a character actor. I later hired him for a part on *Love, American Style*. By the way he reacted, you would have thought I had given him the moon. After that we would talk on the phone every couple of weeks and one day he said, "Well, I bought it." And I said, "What do you mean?" He said, "I have the big C." He died six weeks later of stomach cancer.

Even though Ed and I never made it as a comedy team, he encouraged me to pursue my own career with his absolute love for show business. The highlight of his acting career was a small part as a bookie in the movie *The Sting*. Even though he had parts here and there, his career never took off. But Ed was never frustrated or disappointed by losing a part or suffering rejection, because he was so happy being a part of the profession. A bitter word never came from his mouth. I've never seen anybody who had quite the affair with this business as Ed did. It was that kind of dedication that I would always find so irresistible when I discovered it in other actors. Later I think one of my strengths as a director was that I loved actors and their tenacity so damned much. Ed was one of the first actors I admired.

Once Ed and I split up, I went out on my own, taking jobs as master of ceremonies. Just when I was starting to convince myself that maybe I had the talent for solo performing, it became clear that I didn't have the stomach for it. I didn't have the burning desire to eat all the crap that the business had to serve. Great comedians like Jack Carter, Jack Benny, and George Burns all came from very poor backgrounds and were driven to risk it all on stage. But I wasn't ready to dedicate the rest of my life to performing on the comedy circuit. I knew that there was something else out there that was me, because performing clearly wasn't it.

After taking a couple of odd jobs, including a stint selling radio time during which I didn't sell a thing, I finally got a dream job in show business. Ironically my father, of all people, was behind it. In September 1953, my father called in his markers from men with names like Mr. G, Three Finger Brown, and Carmine DeSapio, and I got a job as a gofer at CBS. I don't know why my father suddenly changed his mind and decided that it was okay for me to work in television. Perhaps he thought that as long as I wasn't going to be an actual performer, then show business was an acceptable profession.

At the time, CBS was the premiere network and I was going to be paid $40 a week. I was thrilled. I had stepped through the door of television and there would be no going back. I wanted to prove to my father and to myself that life could be a little easier and a lot happier for me than it had been for him. I didn't have to go to work every morning full of rage and anxiety with my fists clenched. Things would be different for me. I couldn't wait to go to a cocktail party and have someone ask me where I worked and answer proudly, "CBS."

I was about to get my first taste of the drug called television.

2.

From Gofer to Director
in Five Years

Last December I spent the holidays in my Montana house by myself. There I was surrounded by presents, with snow on the roof, but I was all alone inside. I have vowed not to do that again this year. I don't want to feel lonely anymore. I don't want to think about my three failed marriages. I want to surround myself with my daughters, my son-in-law, and my grandson and celebrate life. It's strange because now that I'm not working, now that I may not direct again, there's a certain void in my life that could lead toward even more loneliness. But I'm going to try and fill my time with what brings me the most joy, and it's not the work anymore. It's my family, my friends, and the relationships I've made outside of work.

Despite my pledge to remain upbeat, I've been reading the obituaries lately and I'm starting to recognize more names. Whenever I see someone that I know, I always check their age first. If they are seventy-three or seventy-four years old I breathe a sigh of relief because I figure I still have several years left. But if they are sixty-seven or sixty-nine—any of the years around my age—I begin to get nervous. It's strange to suddenly acknowledge a sense of doom because in the past I'd always been so busy working that doom was a leisure activity. Maybe that's one of the reasons I was always so obsessed with my work. I didn't have time to worry. Or lament. Or turn morbid. I continued to inject a steady fix of my work until I became so high that nothing else mattered. Nothing could bring me down.

Now that I am spending part of my life in Montana, I finally have come down from my high. I'm surprised to find that it's not as terrible as I might have imagined when I was younger. Instead of tension, I've been filling my days with activities like reading and tennis. I went into town today to M & S Meats, the general store where you can do anything from buying a piece of beef to sending a Federal Express package. The store has just about everything but a dating service. The hunters leave their catches outside the front door, so, if you pass by M & S during the winter, you might see a deer lying there with its legs straight up and frozen. M & S dresses and freezes meat and is known world over for its jerky.

One time I went to M & S to pick up some script changes sent by fax from the producers of *Murphy Brown*. As Phyllis, one of the women who works at the store, handed me the fax pages from across the counter, she smiled and said, "Now that's funny." At M & S there's little that goes on unnoticed. As I entered the store today, I remembered the hunters and their frozen catches and thought how different our hobbies are. I play tennis and they hunt. I guess we just have different tastes, but I still find their habits a bit odd. But then again, many people would probably think that the way I made my living in Los Angeles all these years has been pretty odd. In the beginning, I did too.

In the early 1950s, there were no production companies like Lorimar or MTM as there are today. As a result, there was much more freedom as far as job advancement was concerned. It was much easier to rise within the ranks of a network like CBS because there was little or no competition from the outside. A typical path might be to start as a production assistant, move up to production coordinator, then stage manager, assistant director, and so on. It sounds almost unbelievable by today's cutthroat standards, but I started my career in television at CBS as a gofer and stand-in and within five years I was promoted up the ranks to director.

Early in my career I almost got fired because I overslept. I was working at the local CBS affiliate in New York and part of my job was to open up the station in the morning. I would switch on master control, cue the technician to play the "Star Spangled Banner" and the day's scheduled programming would begin. The bottom line was that the station had to be opened and I had the key. One morning I simply overslept (not by much, but by enough). When I woke up and realized what I had done, I jumped out of bed and ran all the way down Park Avenue to the station dressed in my pajamas, a rain coat, and slippers.

It was still pretty early in the morning, so understandably the street was deserted. Suddenly I saw a woman walk out of the Waldorf Tower, where permanent residents came and went through a side entrance to the hotel. When the woman got to the corner, she hailed a cab; that's when I realized it was Marilyn Monroe. I remember thinking first that she was absolutely gorgeous even at dawn, and second that she had a lot of peach fuzz on her face. But I'm sure she didn't think much of me, dashing down the street in my pajamas. I finally made it to the station and opened it up just in time to save the day. From then on, I was early to everything I did. Beginning in live television will do that to a person.

The first TV series I ever worked on at CBS was *Beat the Clock*, the game show where contestants had to do stunts within a certain length of time (usually sixty seconds or less). There were tricks with marshmallows, Jell-O, and hot dogs, and most ended up being pretty messy. If a contestant failed to complete a stunt, he received a penalty, which was often a blast of whipped cream in the face or an entire custard pie. The host was Bud Collyer and we shot the show live in a New York studio called Liederkrantz Hall on 57th Street between Park and Madison Avenues. My job was part stand-in for the actors and part gofer for the cast and crew.

As a stand-in, I literally stood in place of the contestants while the producers tested stunts to gauge their difficulty. More than once my job required me to get a pie in the face. The rest of the time I got coffee, lunch, cigarettes, and dry cleaning for anybody who was above me, (basically everyone). Whether I was catching a pie in the face or delivering coffee, I was happy to be working in television and felt very proud of my job. I thought of myself as an apprentice and learned as much as I could from the people around me.

After *Beat the Clock*, I moved over to a CBS daytime variety series called *The Robert Q. Lewis Show*, where I worked as the stage manager, a job that required me to serve as traffic controller on the sound stage. Lewis was one of the youngest network hosts, known for his horn-rimmed black glasses and bad skin. While I was working as the stage manager, the show held auditions for a delivery boy, who was to become a running character on the series. The part called for a young man to barge in on the show, no matter who was singing or dancing, and say crazy things like, "I have a sandwich for Rupert Q. Lumis." Then Lewis and the delivery boy would slide right into a skit and discuss weird sandwiches, coffee you could cut with a scissors, and other outlandish take-out orders.

Despite auditioning many people, the producers couldn't find an actor to play the delivery boy. I can't remember whose idea it was, but out of the blue I was asked to audition. And as quickly as I auditioned, I was told the part was mine. I started appearing once, then twice, and eventually three times a week. I was earning $132 a week as stage manager and suddenly was getting between $400 and $800 a week as an actor. My transition to acting left me feeling extremely fortunate. I was on a roll. The only fly in the ointment was that Lewis could sometimes be a terror.

There was a teleprompter in his desk, and during a scene we could both read off of it. We would do the first skit, which I usually had memorized, and then the action would stop before we went to a commercial. The shows aired live in those days, so tension was higher when the cameras were rolling. One day during a commercial break, Lewis screamed at me, "Why didn't you go to the end of the bit? Couldn't you look at my eyes? I was trying to get you to go to the end of the bit!" He screamed and yelled at me in front of the audience, and then as soon as we came back from the commercial, he turned on a dime and said, "That was Al Rafkin. Isn't he wonderful, folks?" I walked off the stage that day with a headache that could have killed a rhino.

Lewis also would throw tantrums. He'd slam his dressing-room door so hard behind him that it would get stuck and he couldn't get out. After the show I would stand with some of the crew in the alley outside the studio and laugh like hell as we watched Lewis climb out the bathroom window of his dressing room. Despite Lewis's erratic behavior, I had a lot of fun on that show, especially with the other members of the cast. Although there were many guest performers, the regular male singer was Merv Griffin (who often had us over to his apartment for parties) and the female singer was Jaye P. Morgan (a delightful and very funny woman). The pit band was run by Ray Block and included many top-notch musicians. Overall, it was a truly talented bunch.

When I started the Lewis show it was shot in black and white but eventually, like many other shows of the time, we started shooting once a week in color. The producers would send us all down to another studio where they would put weird makeup on us like black lipstick and very heavy pancake powder. And as if Lewis wasn't bizarre-looking enough, with the makeup on he really looked like a circus clown. We were on the verge of a new production process, but it all looked pretty garish to me.

While I was performing as the delivery boy on the *Lewis* show, I met a CBS executive named Lou Stone who seemed excited about my future as an actor. One day he called me into his office and said that he had seen me on the show and loved it. He said, "I want to shoot a pilot with your delivery boy as the star. We're going to build a whole show around you." Needless to say, I was thrilled and more than a little shocked. But I hardly had time to get used to the idea before I heard Lou had committed suicide by throwing himself out of a window in the Vanderbilt Hotel. I think that's probably when I realized that this business was even more precarious than I'd originally thought.

Eventually, the *Robert Q. Lewis Show* was canceled, and we were all wondering where we would land next. Everyone was pretty nervous, except for Merv Griffin. He went back to his apartment and played the piano. He always knew something good was going to happen to him. (And years later, it turned out he was right. His game show empire produced such hits as *Jeopardy* and *Wheel of Fortune* and made Merv a zillionaire.)

I was still on the CBS payroll so I knew I would have little trouble finding another job. I decided to take a vacation before moving on. I went to southern California, where I fell instantly and madly in love with a cocktail waitress. It was the first time in my life that I was totally smitten sexually. This woman turned me inside out. She could do marvelous and wonderful things for me. I was with her when I got a call to go back to New York and become the stage manager on a new show called *Captain Kangaroo*. I went from hot sex to children's programming in the length of one phone call.

On the first day of *Captain Kangaroo*, the president of CBS, Louis Cowan, came down to the stage. It was very early in the morning and I overheard him talking to the Captain, Bob Keeshan. Cowan said, "Be gentle and don't yell at the children." Cowan didn't need to caution Keeshan; the man knew exactly what he was doing. When we went on the air that morning we all felt something special, and children and parents soon agreed. Keeshan had a mythical and magical quality about him from day one.

On *Captain Kangaroo* our day began around three A.M. with rehearsal. Starting at eight o'clock we would perform one hour live for the East Coast audience. Then we'd take a forty-second station break and turn around and do the whole show again for the West Coast. I was in charge of the stage, making sure the next segment was ready to go whether it involved a live performer, farm animal, or puppet. I stood on the stage wearing ear phones so I could hear the assistant director in the booth coordinating the action between the cameras and actors.

The show's menagerie of characters included Grandfather Clock, Dancing Bear, and Bunny Rabbit. The bunny puppet was run by Cosmo Allegretti, who was then rather tumultuously married to actress Carol Lawrence (who was rumored to be cheating on Cosmo with actor Howard Keel). I used to hear the assistant director calling out, "Cue the bunny on the rainbow." Cosmo would sit the bunny on a rainbow and the cameras would push in. When I heard the cue for the first time, it made me realize that television is probably the silliest and most wonderful business in the world. In what other line of work would such a funny phrase have such significance?

I also enjoyed working with Hugh (Lumpy) Brannum, who was the unforgettable Mr. Green Jeans. He was always the one who played with the animals, and he didn't even seem to mind the smell of baby sheep at three in the morning. During one show we had some lion cubs on, and one of them bit two of Brannum's fingers. Because the show was live, there was little we could do to intervene without blowing the show. Like a real trooper, Brannum kept his hand in his pocket for the entire show. Blood was streaming down his pants leg, but he stayed in character until the end.

We had a great supporting cast, but everybody knew the main reason for *Captain Kangaroo*'s more than twenty years of success was Keeshan. He was simply mesmerizing when he would look into the camera and talk directly to the children. Toward the end of each episode he would sit in a rocking chair and say a helpful reminder like, "Be good to mommy today," or "Remember to say please and thank you." One day Peter Birch, the director of the show, was instructing a camera man to pull back away from the shot. But the camera man said, "I can't. The Captain has his legs locked around the camera." And sure enough, Bob was rocking back and forth in the chair with his boots firmly wrapped around the camera's pedestal. He had a big smile on his face as the delightful theme music faded in to take us off the air.

I stayed on *Captain Kangaroo* a couple of years and made some good friends. The crew, some of whom had done stage work, were in television and loving it. The good money, steady hours, and sense of job security made it a happy time for many of us. But as with some stars who face the challenges of success, Keeshan became a little cranky. But on-camera, Keeshan was a professional. He really did care about his audience, and remains a strong child advocate.

After *Captain Kangaroo* I became an assistant director on a CBS series called *The Verdict Is Yours*, which was one of television's first courtroom dramas. The host was Jim McKay, who would later become the icon of ABC's *Wide World of Sports*. The show centered around reenactments of legal trials, using real-life lawyers and judges along with a changing cast of actors who played the witnesses, defendants, and plaintiffs. I remember that the stories were extremely well written.

Each actor was given his background and relationship to the case and he could only improvise within that framework. An actor could hem and haw, but he couldn't alter the basic facts of his character as written. A lot of actors couldn't do this at all, while others could do it exceptionally well. The jury was composed of members from the studio audience, and McKay served as the court reporter to provide trial background and play-by-play. At the end of the trial, which might last as long as five days, the jury would deliberate. When the verdict was announced, some actors took it very personally. If one lost a case you might overhear him saying, "What will I tell my agent?"

When actors came in to audition, I used to keep notes on them for my own amusement. Some went on to have very successful careers in television and film. I remember when Richard Chamberlain came in to audition I wrote, "Maybe the worst actor I've heard this year." Some actors find it easy to improvise, but I thought Chamberlain made it look like drudgery. He was just plain bad. But shortly after that Richard moved to London where he took additional acting classes and turned into the fine performer he is today.

One of the most delightful things about working on *The Verdict* was being around Jim McKay. He was bright, charming, and best of all, shorter than me. Our clothing sense also was compatible: Neither one of us was a very snappy dresser. One day Jim drove up to the studio in his convertible wearing a brand new sports cap, like the kind you see English men wearing when they drive their Morgans down country roads. Jim stepped out of his car and looked quite the fashion plate.

I said, "Jim, you look great. The combination of that hat with that car is perfect!"

He smiled and turned to walk into the studio. That's when I saw the price tag to his hat hanging over his left ear.

After *The Verdict Is Yours,* I continued to climb the CBS ladder when I moved up to associate producer on a series hosted by the legendary Arthur Godfrey. In the 1950s, Godfrey was to television what Oprah Winfrey is today. In fact, he was probably even bigger than Oprah. If he announced on his show that he thought everybody should lose five pounds, then the country would lose five pounds. It was as simple as that.

After finding incredible success on radio in the 1940s, Godfrey moved to television with such top-rated hits in the 1950s as *Arthur Godfrey's Talent Scouts* (a precursor to today's *Star Search*) and a musical variety show called *Arthur Godfrey and His Friends*, where he sat behind a desk (like today's Jay Leno and David Letterman). Regulars on the latter show included the Chordettes, Frank Parker, Marion Marlowe, and Julius LaRosa, who Godfrey later fired on the air saying he had gotten to be too big a star.

In the beginning, Godfrey was the hottest guy on television, and the press chronicled and applauded his every move. But that's not when I worked for him. I knew him toward the end of his career, when things began to sour. The press started to vilify him for, among other things, the heartless way he fired his supporting cast one by one. The Godfrey I knew, quite frankly, was a bigoted and mean human being. He was one of the meanest men I have ever met, but few people knew it because he hid behind a well-manufactured mask of deception. To his audience he was the celebrity who smiled into the camera. Behind the scenes, he was a man who hurled racial slurs and insults without any hesitation.

When I was associate producer on *Arthur Godfrey and His Friends*, I had a good job, despite the star's attitude and waning popularity. Well, most of the time it was a good job, except for the time I almost got Godfrey involved in a lawsuit. That day we welcomed Eddie Hodges, a little boy who was then appearing in *The Music Man* on Broadway. We had planned to have him perform the famous "Inch Worm" song on the show with Godfrey, but the writers on our show decided they wanted to spice it up and rewrote the lyrics, calling it "Book Worm."

We shot the show and everything went off beautifully except for one hitch: I had forgotten to clear the lyric changes with song writer Frank Loesser, who was then one of Broadway's brightest talents. I thought Loesser was going to sue Godfrey, and my career in television would end over a silly song about an inch worm. My fledgling career was given a reprieve when Godfrey intervened and smoothed Loesser's ruffled feathers by, I assume, writing a check. Needless to say, I never again forgot to clear a set of song lyrics. Ever.

The time I spent with Godfrey was significant for me because I was able to see, first hand, how a man handles fame on his way down. One day producer Billy Hammerstein and I walked into the makeup room and Godfrey was sitting in a chair. From the back you could see that this big hulk of a man was sobbing. He said, "I'm going out with my tail between my legs. I should have quit when I was a success." Although I felt sorry for him, inside I also was nodding my head and saying, "You got what you deserved, pal." Oddly enough, the end of Godfrey's career marked the beginning of my own as a director.

One day on the Godfrey set I got a call from an executive at CBS asking if I would like to direct one of their public service shows. These shows were programs the Federal Communications Commission required networks to do and were often religious or service programming like *Look Up and Live* and *Lamp unto My Feet*. To make their point about humanity, some of the shows would use jazz artists and gospel singers such as Mahalia Jackson and Ella Fitzgerald. I told CBS that I really wanted to be a director and that I would be happy to do it. I had to start somewhere and these shows seemed as good a place as any.

Word of my decision to take a directing job quickly got back to Godfrey. He came into my office and said, "I understand that you're leaving." We had barely said ten words to each other in the six months that I had been around, but now suddenly he wanted to have a heart-to-heart talk. He sat in my office and proceeded to lecture me on everything from how to raise children to how to plow a furrow. And then he wished me well and left. I think he just wanted to see if he still had the power to mesmerize someone with his words. Sad but true.

So my career as a television director was off and running. The service shows again were live, and aired early Sunday morning. Like *Captain Kangaroo,* we went to work at 3:00 or 3:30 A.M. and rehearsed until 5:30 or 6:00 A.M. It was such a weird time to be heading into work.

There I was walking down the street and I'd pass by fellows kissing their dates goodnight. I even got mugged once, which seemed bizarre because I was on my way to direct a religious program. Despite the hour, the shows were perfect for my first job as a director. That's not to say I didn't walk around with a stomach full of nerves most of the time, but I knew I was getting a solid directing education. I was working with talented actors (including Eli Wallach and Anne Jackson) and first-rate musicians and singers (most of whom were working for scale). For that kind of training, it was even worth getting up so early in the morning.

▗▄▄▄▄▄▄▄▄▖

After directing the religious shows, I started to look for freelance assignments outside of the CBS umbrella. It was time for me to see what else I could do. In May 1960 producers Joe and Gil Cates hired me to direct the television broadcast of Ringling Bros. and Barnum and Bailey Circus with host Bert Parks. When I was growing up, my father had often taken me to Madison Square Garden to see the rodeo, which I had found absolutely enchanting and considered one of the thrills of my childhood. But I had never seen a circus performance. Obviously, I didn't let the Cates brothers know that. I told them to sign me up. I was ready. A job was a job, and I wanted to see if I could do it.

We were to shoot the show in Greensboro, North Carolina, but I first flew down to Miami Beach where the circus was on tour. In those days direct airline flights were the exception. We did what seemed like fourteen take-offs and landings between New York and Miami Beach. I went with my line producer Tony Ford, who was Catholic and crossed himself before every take-off. I thought, if it was good enough for him, it was good enough for me. So I did the same and still do to this day, even though I'm Jewish.

We did make it and arrived in time to catch the star of the circus, acrobat Harold Alzonna, who did what he called the "Slide for Life." He climbed up a wire (which was set at a huge incline), got to the top (some seventy or eighty feet in the air), and then slid down backwards. The trick was breathtaking and all I had to do was capture it on film.

I was ready for anything except for the fact that when we arrived in North Carolina, Harold Alzonna was nowhere to be found. He left Miami with the circus, but failed to show up in Greensboro with the rest of the troupe. No one could explain his disappearance. Then, to make matters more confusing, it snowed for two days in Greensboro, which was very unusual. It paralyzed the whole city. Nobody even had a shovel in the town. I thought for sure nobody was going to come out to see the circus. Why would they? There was a snowdrift blocking the entrance, and we had no star.

The day before the show, we finally found Harold sitting on a Greensboro street corner bare-chested and drunk. We sobered him up and got him ready to rehearse. Then I took the technical director up with me on the cat walk, which was a little narrow aisle made of iron mesh that stood high above the arena. As I looked down through the holes in the mesh, my knees turned to jelly. The technical director had to help me crawl back down on my hands and knees. I hadn't known until that very moment that I was afraid of heights. What else could possibly go wrong?

Despite the snow, losing Harold, and my fear of heights, we went on with the show. Before the broadcast, I gathered together the whole cast and crew and complimented them on how much I had enjoyed working with them (even with all of our problems). They were true professionals and it was a pleasure to be in their company. Suddenly, they started to applaud me, and I remember looking out and being quite shocked. Later somebody told me it was a European custom among circus performers. But whatever it was, it certainly was a treat for me and gave me a real sense of pride as a director. I was beaming.

Working with the circus performers was like being part of a huge family, and I hadn't felt that warmth since my Sunday night dinners with the Billeras back in Pennsylvania. The performers were not only polite, but they worked their fannies off. They were constantly practicing, especially the young people, who weren't even appearing before an audience yet. They rehearsed for hours and hours. Like actors, the circus people knew the key to performing was rehearsing. They simply defined the phrase "a professional family," and gave me an enormous amount of respect for life under the big top.

▬ ▰ ▰ ▰ ▲

While I was marketing myself as a freelance director, I got a call that would be the most pivotal phone call of my career. The producers of *The Verdict Is Yours* were moving the show from New York to Los Angeles, and the current director, Byron Paul, didn't want to make the move. They called me and said, "Because you used to be the assistant director on the show, would you like to move to California and become the director?" I was a single, thirty-one-year-old guy who was being offered a job in California. It seemed like nirvana to me.

On June 6, 1960, I flew to California and landed at the airport in Los Angeles. I got off the plane and went to the cab stand. The cab driver got out of the car, came around the side, and opened the back door for me. I stood there stunned. In New York you practically had to chase a cab down a street, and here I was looking at a driver holding the door open for me like I was an important person. I knew immediately that I was in love with California.

On my first day at CBS, I was introduced to Lily LaCava, the woman who would be my production assistant and secretary. She was only four-feet-ten-inches tall and just a darling lady. I worked with her from the 1960s up until her death in 1992 when I was directing the sitcom *Coach*. The last time I saw Lily was when I went to visit her in the hospital. She had a brain tumor, and I think we both knew that she didn't have very long to live. But she smiled up at me from her hospital bed and said cheerfully, "I'll be back to work on Monday." She died shortly after that. Lily also worked on and off as a script supervisor, and as long as I knew her, she never shared very much about her personal life. I knew she had never married, but she had the biggest heart I've ever known (and the largest wardrobe). Lily was simply a great lady.

So, there I was in Hollywood working as a director with an assistant and everything. California was looking better than New York by the minute. The first place I lived in Los Angeles was an apartment on

Lexington Avenue and it was not in one of Hollywood's better sections. Gorgeous George, once a famous wrestler, lived there, as well as a lot of ex-starlets with faces that were familiar yet ultimately forgettable. The apartment complex looked like a one-story motel inhabited by guys with tattoos and women with large breasts. It was like a bad Tennessee Williams play. At first, I was a little uncomfortable and sometimes felt like I was living on another planet, but my parents didn't need to know that. For once in my life, they were proud of me because I was making a good living. I left out all the seedy details when I called or wrote home.

Another thing my parents didn't need to know about was my sexual marathon. There were so many beautiful women in Hollywood and it was such an exciting time to be working in the business that I just couldn't help myself. I was like a kid in a candy store. If a woman stood still long enough, we had an affair. It had only been a few years since I had been getting pies in the face on *Beat the Clock,* and now I was being invited to parties hosted by Eddie Fisher and Elizabeth Taylor. More than once I woke up in some woman's apartment and wasn't quite sure where I'd met her, but was pretty sure of what I had done. My sexual escapades came to a halt when I met a woman named Ann Rosin.

I knew Ann for three months and then I married her. Just like that. I obviously didn't know her very well because three months is hardly enough time to do such a thing. She worked as a secretary and assistant in the garment industry. Even though she wasn't in show business and we were young, we were very much in love (or so we thought) and marriage seemed like a logical step. Ann later gave birth to our first daughter, Dru, and several years after that we adopted our second daughter, Leigh. From the moment the girls entered my life, they brought magic into it. The marriage to Ann, however, was a different story.

From the beginning our marriage was not terrific, and I take great responsibility for that. I didn't give myself a chance to get to know Ann. Eventually, when we did get to know each other, we realized that we didn't have anything in common, least of all our senses of humor. We were divorced by 1970. Ironically, we get along much better now that we aren't married. Some relationships just are that way. But I don't regret a moment of the marriage because we raised two magnificent daughters who continue to make me prouder each day.

■ ▬ ▬ ▬ ▲

Although my married life got off on an impulsive path, my directing career took a straighter and steadier road. Along with the original director of *The Verdict Is Yours,* the show's host, Jim McKay, didn't want to move to California either. I thought this was incredibly courageous on Jim's part, because he didn't have another job lined up. But his wife, Maggie, was a columnist on the East Coast, and they had set up a nice life for themselves in Connecticut. Jim did agree, however, to come out to Los Angeles for two weeks to help get us started and ease the transition. After Jim left, we replaced him with a new host named Bill Stout, who was a newsman on the local CBS affiliate. (Two days later, Jim was hired by ABC sports in New York.)

Bill was one of the old-style journalists who would go out and dig up his own story, as opposed to the pompadour blow-dried boy and girl news readers we have today (who try so hard to be cute you could puke). Stout was a real trench-coat kind of guy and I loved him. He was so bright and said what was on his mind, particularly when he'd had a cocktail or two. He once came to our house for dinner, had a couple of drinks, and made a pass at my wife, Ann. I forgave him because he was one of those people who turned into a thirteen-year-old when he drank.

Directing *The Verdict Is Yours* was a wonderful time for me. I liked the crew, the actors, and particularly the real-life district attorneys and judges on the show, who took everything very seriously. We shot the series in Los Angeles from 1960 until late 1962, and then we were canceled. Just like that I went from my role as the director of a television show to a new role on the unemployment line. It wasn't like the old days when I would just move over to another CBS show. Being a director was a whole different game.

Things also were different for me personally because I had more responsibility. By 1962, I had a wife and a baby to support. I started to panic a little until one day Bill Stout came through for me. He went to a cocktail party and was talking to television producer Sheldon Leonard. At the time Leonard and his partner Danny Thomas were producing the top situation comedies on the air. At the party, Sheldon was bemoaning the fact that there were no good comedy directors around. He was looking to train a whole new crop. Stout, who had always enjoyed my sense of humor, mentioned my name. Leonard said, "Well, send him up."

I was about to enter the world of sitcoms that would take hold of my life and not let go for the next thirty-four years, for better or for worse. And frankly, I would see a lot of both.

3.

Tales of Mayberry
and Jeannie in a Bottle

In Montana I am building a guest cottage adjacent to my house so there will be more room for my daughters and their growing families when they visit. The man I hired to build the addition likes to shoot elk with a bow and arrow on the weekends. Sometimes when I think of my neighbors who brandish weapons, it dawns on me how little I have in common with them. But most of the time, oddly enough, I feel quite comfortable here.

When I first bought the land and built this house in late 1991, most of my friends in Hollywood didn't think I would last six weeks. But I've proved them all wrong, and with little effort. It's been more than five years now, averaging six months a year, and I'm still going strong. I recently was the commencement speaker at the local Polson High School graduation, after being asked to participate by a neighbor whose son was graduating. Before and after my speech I got to visit with many of the local families and their children. The afternoon was like something out of a Norman Rockwell painting, with families and with men wearing short-sleeved shirts and suspenders. I was so glad to be a part of it.

The parents of the graduating seniors took out ads in the town newspaper congratulating their children. Many of the ads included pictures of the kids as toddlers in embarrassing poses like on the potty or peeing on the front lawn. What amazed me was to see how many times the word "love" was mentioned in the parents' ad copy. The honest and blatant show of affection surprised and delighted me. Some people might find where we live rather straitlaced and dull, but it's a fascinating thing to be able to see the process of parents raising wonderful children. It's simple and remarkable.

I suppose it's the sheer simplicity of life up here that makes me so content and reminds me of a time when television was simpler. Looking back on the shows I directed during the 1960s, one might refer to them derogatorily as "too wholesome" or "corny." But I look back on them with admiration because they were produced by people who cared about their shows, performed by actors who were proud of their work, and watched by families who sat down together and enjoyed them. Like the Polson parents, these shows were filled with love. In the last few years some people have advised me not to put *The Andy Griffith Show* on my résumé because it will be looked down on with disdain and ageism. But back in the 1960s, it was a credit anyone would have acknowledged with pride. I certainly did, and I still do today.

My introduction to Sheldon Leonard was a wonderful opportunity for my directing career. Eventually he and partner Danny Thomas would nearly dominate the air waves with sitcoms like *The Andy Griffith Show, Gomer Pyle, U.S.M.C., The Joey Bishop Show, The Danny Thomas Show,* and *The Dick Van Dyke Show.* The old Desilu-Cahuenga studio had, I think, nine soundstages and Sheldon and Danny had a show filming on every one.

Taking a meeting with Sheldon was like being interviewed by a gangster, because he had played so many on film and television. Beyond his thick Brooklyn accent and street-wise demeanor, however, there was a brilliant director-producer and a fine man. During our first meeting, he pontificated about sitcom and its similarities to Greek tragedy, and then hired me to join a directors' training program. The other directors hired along with me were Lee Philips, Coby Ruskin, and Hal Cooper. None of us had ever directed situation comedy before, but I can't think of a better place to learn than Sheldon and Danny's stables.

The first thing we did as a group was go down to the set of *The Dick*

Van Dyke Show and observe director John Rich in action. Rich was a bull of a man with a voice to match, and I adored him. He was so generous with us and even jokingly taught us how to take away his job (which was silly because none of us ever could). But apparently whatever we learned from being around John for a few weeks was good enough to get us all jobs on other sitcoms. Sheldon farmed us each out to a different series, and I landed on *Make Room for Daddy*, starring Danny Thomas. I was thirty-two years old, and about to direct my first sitcom starring a comedic legend. I tried not to think about the weight of my new position too much because I didn't want to be the one to trip first.

On a sitcom, the one thing a director prays for every week is a well-written script. If the story is nicely constructed, then you can see the scenes unfold like a piece of film in your mind. If the script is good, you can sail through the week of staging the scenes with the actors and crew. If the script is bad, it can be like slogging through mud. It doesn't matter if it's shot one camera (as most sitcomes were in the 1960s), three cameras (like in the 1970s through 1990s), or a dozen cameras, mud is mud. But if you work with the writers enough, you can firm up some of the mud. Although I was new to sitcom directing, I felt I could already recognize a good script from a bad, and hopefully would have more of the latter. That gave me confidence.

I had always adored Danny Thomas and considered him to be one of the great storytellers of all time. I wasn't intimidated by him because he really wasn't the kind of man who set out to intimidate others. He was gracious to me, but oddly enough he never called me by my name—first or last. Now that I think about it, I don't think he knew my name. He would call out, "Hey, director" or "Mr. Director." He always had a smile on his face when he called me, but I think if he had been pressed he wouldn't have been able to come up with "Alan Rafkin." Even though he didn't know my name, I'd like to think he respected my work. If there had been a problem, I'm sure I would have heard about it.

Working on *Make Room for Daddy* (later renamed *The Danny Thomas Show*) was a lovely experience because I was getting a chance to work with the best in television. The cast had wonderful concentration, except for a quirky young actor named Rusty Hamer, who played

Danny's sitcom son. Whenever we were shooting a scene and the punch line was coming up, Rusty would start to smile and, obviously, give the joke away every time. Whenever I would take him aside to discuss the problem, he would wax wise with me and say like a veteran actor, "Don't worry. I'll give it to you on air." But on air, sure enough, he would do it again. Danny would shoot me a look like, "Are you going to get him or am I?"

I loved directing *Make Room for Daddy*, but just when everything seemed to be going so well, I fumbled my career. One night I did something (I can't remember specifically what it was) that upset Sheldon, leading him to yell at me in front of the cast and crew. No matter what I had done, I didn't think it was appropriate for Sheldon, the producer of the show, to yell at me in front of everyone. I thought he should have taken me aside and quietly reprimanded me. But he didn't, and I thought it made me lose the respect of the cast and crew.

After finishing the show that night, some of the cast members and I went for a late dinner at La Scala in Beverly Hills. When we arrived at the restaurant, Sheldon and his wife Frankie were sitting at a booth. When he saw us, Sheldon gave our group a friendly wave. Still smarting from having been taken out by him on the stage, I snubbed him by rolling my eyes at his gesture. From that one snub, I didn't work in television for the next eight months. It was my first lesson on industry politics. I realized the hard way that there were people who ran the business and if you didn't play by their rules, you didn't play at all.

Eventually, I was accepted back into the sitcom fold. My agent at the time was William Morris, who also represented Danny and Sheldon. I guess after eight months my agent convinced them that I had suffered long enough. All was forgiven and I was welcomed back with a plum assignment: *The Dick Van Dyke Show*. Some of the funniest episodes of any television sitcom I've ever done were on that series.

One of my favorites was a show in which Dick accidentally gets hypnotized at a dinner party. For the rest of the show, whenever he hears a bell ring, he acts drunk; and whenever a bell rings a second time, he sobers up. He continues to change between drunk and sober when a typewriter dings, a telephone rings, and on and on. The script called for a lot of physical comedy for the segments when Dick was drunk, and he was magnificent. The idea for the show came from a bit Dick used to do in his nightclub act: A guy comes home drunk and every time his wife looks at him, he sobers up.

I directed nearly a dozen episodes of *The Dick Van Dyke Show* and each show just got better and better. (Mary Tyler Moore was also a pleasure to work with, but I would get to know her much better a few years later when I directed *The Mary Tyler Moore Show*.) While I was directing Dick's series, I shot one episode of *The Andy Griffith Show*, which was at the height of its popularity. The show was not only loved by viewers, but it quickly became my personal all-time favorite sitcom.

It was around 1964 and sitcoms were shot with a single camera, taking about three days to complete. It was similar to a movie and I loved the fact that it only took us three days (as opposed to the week-long schedules I would later work on three-camera sitcoms). At the end of my first day on the job, Andy Griffith walked over to me.

"You like this, don't you?" asked Andy.

"Yes," I said.

"Would you like to do more of these?"

"Sure."

"How would you like to do the rest of the season?"

My stomach flipped out of my body, and I had to reach across the stage to pull it back in. I immediately answered Andy with a monumental "Yes." I went on to direct the series for more than two years. It remains the happiest time in my career. The cast was simply the most professional group of people I have ever worked with. I never heard an actor complain, whine, or even wince at a scene. It was television sitcom at its finest and I couldn't believe that I was a part of it all. *The Andy Griffith Show*'s weekly adventures in Mayberry were a metaphor for everything I had come to respect and relish about television production.

To top it all off, Andy was one of the most decent people I'd ever known. He was perpetually smiling and usually it was because of something Don Knotts had done to make him laugh. (In fact the only person I ever knew that Andy didn't get along with was Jack Burns,

The cast of *The Dick Van Dyke Show*. Dick Van Dyke, Mary Tyler Moore, Rose Marie, me as director, producer-writer Carl Reiner, Morey Amsterdam, and Jerry Paris. *Courtesy of Calvada Productions.*

who came on to play Barney Fife's cousin after Don left the show. Andy knew nobody could ever replace Don.) When Andy wasn't laughing, he was supervising the scripts. He would spend his hiatus going over every single script for the next season along with producer Bob Ross, a talented man who never got in my way when it came to directing. By the time we got the scripts right before rehearsal, they were already in good shape. We would get up on our feet and make very few changes.

The set of *The Andy Griffith Show* was as pleasant as the town of Mayberry. In between takes, when we were lighting a shot, Andy would play his guitar and Lee Greenwood, his makeup artist, would play the banjo. We would all sing along, or Don Knotts might perform a comic monologue. (I remember one in particular about a Country Western disc jockey that was hysterical and quite obscene.) Then, Friday night

A caricature of me drawn by
Dick Van Dyke on the back of
a script, 1963. *Courtesy of Alan
Rafkin.*

when we'd finish shooting, we'd go to Frascatti's, a popular restaurant
and legendary Frank Sinatra hangout. We'd drink a lot, eat a lot, and go
home and have a wonderful weekend. It was nothing but a dream job
from A to Z.

Another joy of *The Andy Griffith Show* was working with a
young Ron Howard. It's never been a surprise to me that Ron
Howard has gone on to become a successful movie director. When
he was six years old and you asked him what he wanted to be when
he grew up, he would say "a director." He came from a very neat
family of actors, including his mother, father, and brother. It was
quite common for little Ronny to watch me direct the series with

On the set of *The Andy Griffith Show* with Don Knotts on the left, and Andy Griffith and George "Goober" Lindsey. *Courtesy of Paramount Pictures. The Andy Griffith Show. Copyright © 1960 by Paramount Pictures. All Rights Reserved.*

more than the usual childhood interest. Acting was only a stepping-stone for this boy.

One of his parents was on the set at all times. Whenever I looked over to either his mom or dad, they would be sitting there with a smile, just so pleased with everything they were watching. They were simply content and happy for their son. The only request they ever made was for occasional time off for Ron to attend his little league baseball games. They would ask very politely a week in advance, and we'd always comply. They were the antithesis of the meddling stage parents you hear about today.

Some directors don't like to work with child actors because they can be difficult, but Ron was always considered an asset rather than a liability on *The Andy Griffith Show*. Whenever the script called for a "heart scene," or a sentimental moment between Opie Taylor and his

Pa, the acting was a particular treat to watch. Ron could bring so much emotion to the scene that even during the rehearsals I could see that Andy was tightening his jaw trying not to cry. Ron had a great effect on Andy, and Andy adored him as well. Ron simply is one of those exceptional young people who grows up to be an exceptional adult.

Years later when I was directing the TV series *Coach* on the Universal lot, I learned that Ron was nearby directing his movie *Apollo 13*. One morning I got a call from Ron's assistant saying that Ron had seen me on the lot and wondered if I would like to come over and visit him on the set of his movie. I hadn't seen him in years. He's now a balding father of four, but still has that same gracious, smiling face. He couldn't have been nicer to me when I visited him. We walked from one set to another, and he told me what fond memories he had of our times together on *The Andy Griffith Show.*

For a sitcom director, there are often shows that you look back on with anxiety and angst. With *The Andy Griffith Show* there was never that, and the experience spoiled me for other sitcoms that would be nothing but trouble. Andy showed me what it could be like to work on a series and really enjoy myself. We did our work and we did it as a real team, taking our cues from Andy who was gentle, sweet, and very considerate. If I sound overly complimentary, it's only because those qualities are not the kind you find in the stars of most television series.

One of the best ways to tell if a show is truly successful is its ability to spin off other shows. *The Andy Griffith Show* was powerful enough not only to run on its own steam for more than eight years, but also to spin off two other television programs: *Gomer Pyle, U.S.M.C.* and *Mayberry, R.F.D.* (a successor sitcom when Andy left the cast). The Gomer Pyle series was created thanks to the following Jim Nabors had built for himself on Andy's show. Andy and his manager had discovered Jim Nabors singing in a Santa Monica nightclub and hired him to play Gomer Pyle, an attendant at Wally's gas station.

One day we were shooting a scene of *The Andy Griffith Show* outside the Desilu-Cahuenga studio gates in Hollywood. Andy and Don were sitting in a police car while we were lighting the shot, when suddenly Jim Nabors came running over with a piece of paper in his hand. "We beat you! We beat you!" he shouted with glee. He was showing

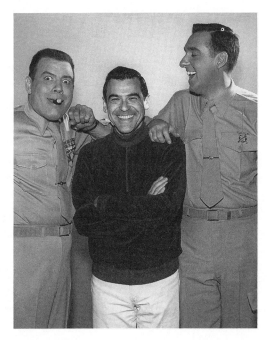

On the set of *Gomer Pyle, U.S.M.C.*, flanked by the
late Frank Sutton and Jim Nabors. *Courtesy of
Paramount Pictures. Gomer Pyle, U.S.M.C. Copyright
© 1964 by Paramount Pictures. All Rights Reserved.*

Andy the current weeks' ratings during which *Gomer Pyle* had beaten
The Andy Griffith Show. Jim Nabors doesn't have a mean bone in his
body, but the look on Andy's face wasn't exactly happiness for a fellow
competitor. He was hurt. It's one thing to help another actor launch a
sitcom and be happy for him; it's another for the sitcom to surpass your
own. Thankfully, Andy and Jim are friends today now that the competition is over.

After directing *The Andy Griffith Show,* I temporarily left television
for the only time in my life to direct several movies with Don Knotts,
who was under contract with Universal Studios. I thought that Andy

would be upset, like I was jumping ship, but it was quite the reverse. He came to visit us on the set of our first movie, *The Ghost and Mr. Chicken,* and he was very supportive. When the *New York Times* reviewed the 1966 film, it said, "It's a picture that UCLA and USC cinema students will be looking at as a classic 20 years from now." Well, the *Times*'s prediction didn't come true, but I loved the movie anyway.

Moviemaking was not quite the leap it might seem as a director, because directing *The Andy Griffith Show* was very similar to directing a movie. We shot both with a single camera and used a master, which is when you set up as much of the scene as is possible with proper staging, and then the camera follows the actors around. One scene may take two or three masters to shoot. You shoot those masters, and then you go back and do the close-ups or what is called coverage to make sure the film editor has everything he needs to put the scene together.

After having worked in television for more than ten years already, switching to film as a change of pace really agreed with me and Don. We didn't have to race through our material the way we did in television. We would rehearse a scene, shoot it, and then I would say, "Don, have you got everything you want out of that bit, or scene?" And he would say, "Yeah. How 'bout you?" If we both signed off on a scene, we would move on. It wasn't rush, rush, rush like in television.

Don was a very kind man, who fans found so accessible and down to earth that they would often ask him to pose for pictures with them outside the commissary at Universal. Don would not only pose for pictures, but would often step behind the camera and take some additional shots of the fans alone. He was a sweet man with very few pretensions: What you saw was what you got with Don.

One day Don and I were eating lunch in the Universal commissary. A man came over to our table, leaned down, and said, "Hi, I'm Cary Grant." He proceeded to tell Don how much he enjoyed his movies. Don, who is basically a very shy man, sat there for several minutes listening to Grant's flattering remarks without saying a word back. Finally, Don mustered up all of his courage and said in a loud voice, "How they treatin' ya?" At the time Cary Grant was probably the highest paid and most famous movie star in all of motion pictures. He smiled, nodded, and said, "Just fine."

Sitting with the nicest and funniest actor I ever worked with, Don Knotts. *Courtesy of Paramount Pictures. The Andy Griffith Show. Copyright © 1960 by Paramount Pictures. All Rights Reserved.*

In addition to *The Ghost and Mr. Chicken*, I also directed Don in a 1968 feature called *The Shakiest Gun in the West*, which was a remake of *Paleface* with Bob Hope. Although our movies had modest budgets (under $1 million apiece), they made respectable profits (from $10 million to $20 million each). As the cards were dealt, I didn't go on to have a major career as a movie director, but I certainly enjoyed the job while it lasted.

After the Don Knotts films, I remained under contract for a short time to Universal. When I wasn't directing, I hung around the lot and still got paid for my time, which was fine with me. One day I was having lunch with actor James Farentino, who was also under contract to Universal at the time. We were eating at the studio commissary when Monique James, a woman who was then in charge of talent at Universal, came over to see us.

"You guys are going to be busy for about fourteen days," she said matter-of-factly.

"What are you talking about?" Farentino asked.

"We're going to do a remake of the film *Man Without a Star*. We'll reshoot the interiors and close-ups with new actors, but keep all the long shots and big horse stunts as is with the old actors. And we'll do it in just fourteen days," she said. "James, you'll play the lead, and Alan will direct."

"That's crazy!" Farentino and I said together. "We won't do it."

"Fine. Then you're both under suspension," she said.

Needless to say we did the movie, a western called *Ride to Hangman's Tree*. But I'll never forget the experience as an example of Universal at its shabbiest. The entire project was motivated by Universal's desire to make money and not movies. It was putting quantity before quality. I've never heard of them doing anything similar since, and I'm certainly happy about that.

Despite that bad experience, the best thing about directing features was that I realized for the first time being a director was the right career for me. And my belief was soon confirmed by others. While directing at Universal, I worked with a movie producer named Ed Montagne. He had done films with Abbott and Costello and was not someone who delivered compliments haphazardly. One day when Montagne was watching me direct, he said, "God damned you're good. You're really good." When he said that I remember being surprised by his effervescent praise, but thinking, "I'm a director and that's exactly where I want to be."

I had the distinction during this time in my career to not only direct Danny Thomas in a sitcom, but his daughter Marlo Thomas as well. I directed several episodes of *That Girl* and found her to be very bright and an ultra-professional. She knew more about looping, editing, camera angles, and music tracks than any actor or actress I'd ever seen before. Her knowledge came from the summers she spent as a child growing up on the Desilu lot. She and her brother and sister were run-

On the set of my first feature film, *Ski Party*, with
in-drag co-stars Dwayne Hickman and Frankie
Avalon. *American International Pictures. Courtesy
of Alan Rafkin.*

ners for their dad's shows, and that's how they learned to know television and love it so well.

During the 1960s I also directed episodes of *The Doris Day Show,
The Patty Duke Show, 77 Sunset Strip, Valentine's Day, Many Happy Re-
turns,* and *Bewitched.* All of those shows were a breeze compared to *The
Cara Williams Show,* which was one of the worst experiences of my life.
At the time, CBS thought that Cara was going to be the next Lucille
Ball. They were wrong.

Because Cara didn't like to come to the set early, we would break
down the production board so she wouldn't need to arrive before
eleven A.M. That wouldn't have been so bad if she had actually showed
up at eleven, but most of the time she strolled in around four o'clock.
She'd usually bring her mother, who would also bring along some of

Directing Marlo Thomas on the set of *That Girl*.
Courtesy of Marlo Thomas.

her friends. Her mother would show her friends around the set and boast, "This is all Cara's. *All* of it." Then her mother would proceed to take home all the Danish and pastries that were set up for the cast and crew.

As far as her personality went, Cara always had a smile pasted on her face. She was never knowingly mean, she just tended to wear people down. She once pushed co-star, Frank Aletter, to his limit and he had to be checked into the hospital with a severe migraine headache. The way things were on the set of *The Cara Williams Show*, it was no shock to any of us when the show folded after one season.

A much more pleasant experience was *The Farmer's Daughter*, based on the film that starred Loretta Young. The television series starred Inger Stevens, with whom I was completely infatuated. Inger was the first lady I worked with who was the boss of her own show, and she was one of the nicest bosses I'd ever met. She was magnificent to look at and good as gold underneath. Inger was always prepared and always such fun. I think we were all shocked later when we heard that she had committed suicide. The story that I got was that she had been in love with an African-American man. It was the 1960s and in those days, particularly if you were a big star, interracial dating was not something that was socially acceptable. I don't know if that's the reason Inger killed herself, but the social pressure on her relationship couldn't have been easy for her.

I again worked with two lovely ladies on *The Donna Reed Show.* Donna had a celebrated motion picture career, and she proved to be equally talented at television. Also on the show was a young actress named Shelley Fabares, whom I have been unashamedly in love with ever since. (Shelley and I teamed up again in the early 1980s on *One Day at a Time,* and in the 1990s on *Coach.*) I was hired to direct one episode of *The Donna Reed Show* because the show's then director, Fred De Cordova, was leaving.

Fred would be remembered best for being the long-time producer of Johnny Carson's *Tonight Show.* Fred, who had worked with Jack Benny, was a very polite and cordial gentleman. As was common then, he introduced me to the cast of *The Donna Reed Show.* It must have been funny to see Fred and me walking around the set together. He looked like a million bucks with an ascot and a beautiful sports jacket. I was wearing my typical directing uniform: sneakers, jeans, and a sweatshirt.

On the first day of *The Donna Reed Show* we blocked out some scenes and had our rehearsal. At the end I said confidently, "Okay, these are the shots. This is the master I want." The cinematographer, who had been watching me all along, leaned over and whispered, "You can't do it. We never shoot Miss Reed from the side you have her facing the camera." She never said a word, but I quickly restaged the scene using another pretext. From then on I was suspicious of the cinematographer. It would have been much kinder if he had told me about Miss Reed's preference before I had wasted our time and effort.

The Donna Reed Show was shot at Screen Gems, where I also directed episodes of *My Favorite Martian* and *I Dream of Jeannie.* My Favorite Martian was a treat because I had admired Ray Walston since seeing him do *Damn Yankees* on Broadway. I read recently that he said he regrets doing *My Favorite Martian* because he was later typecast by the role. But at the time, he was really a joy to work with and didn't show any resentment at all.

Ray's only complaint was about his co-star Bill Bixby. Bill was riding the first bubble of his success and often sat in his dressing room serenading a succession of pretty young women with his ukulele. Ray would come up to me and say, "If he doesn't stop that playing, I'm going to kill him." Aside from the minor tension back stage, the men got along well and seemed to like each other. I had directed about five episodes of the series when producer Jack Popkin called me into his office and announced, "You're fired."

He said the head of CBS thought I was directing Ray Walston "too gay." The comment was ridiculous. Anybody who has ever seen Ray knows that he has unique mannerisms. For example, he doesn't walk; he darts. Also, when he really gets going, he points his arms and hands and moves like a little elf. He's wonderful, and certainly in no way effeminate or gay. He just has his own style.

I told the producer I wasn't doing anything to accentuate Ray's darting, but I was let go anyway. Later when the show became a big hit I was re-hired to direct, but I was still a little sore from being fired in the first place. The few times that I have been let go from a show it has been from the blind side. That's probably the instability of television: When you least expect it, expect trouble.

One of the toughest directing jobs I took during the 1960s was *I Dream of Jeannie*, which starred Larry Hagman, as astronaut Tony Nelson, and Barbara Eden, as a two-thousand-year-old genie who could perform magic. Today the series would be a cinch to produce because of all the new technology in special effects. But back then it was often a struggle. We had to stop and start the camera each time Barbara twisted her nose or folded her arms.

If she wanted someone to disappear, I had to yell, "Freeze." Then Barbara would stop and the person would leave the set. The camera

In between Larry Hagman and Barbara Eden on the set of *I Dream of Jeannie*. *Courtesy of Columbia TriStar Television.*

would keep rolling and then I'd yell, "Action." We'd then continue and everybody left in the room would react to the fact that the person was now gone. When it came time to put the show together, we would edit out the film where the person walked off the stage, and it looked like he or she had disappeared into thin air. The process was extremely anti-quated compared to today's high-tech methods used in such movies as *Star Wars.*

Larry Hagman, who would later head to Southfork and take the helm of a series called *Dallas,* was an edgy and rather neurotic actor. At times he didn't seem to enjoy what he was doing. He was trying to be an actor, and we'd have goats popping in and out and other weird tricks going on. Even though he probably thought it was all rather silly, he was still a hard worker. He came to the set well prepared, knowing all his lines every day.

Bill Daily, who played Tony Nelson's friend Roger Healey, was another story. Bill, who I would later also direct in *The Bob Newhart Show,* used to drive me crazy. If he had a speech more than two sentences long, you could count on ten to thirty takes for him to recite it correctly. He had a terrible time memorizing his lines. In my opinion, he really wasn't cut out to be an actor, but nevertheless, the audience adored him.

Like Hagman, Barbara Eden was well polished when it came to her work in front of the camera. She was always so prepared and one of the most professional women I've ever known. At the time I also admired the fact that she was balancing the starring role in a series with the starring role as a mother to her young son. I can spot a phony parent from miles away, but Barbara was just terrific with her son. I think that's what I liked best about her. She always had the time and stamina to be prepared for both parts.

I also directed a number of *Get Smart* episodes. The first assignment I had on the series was to shoot a scene on a lake with mist around it. In those days we did most of the exteriors on the back lot of the CBS Radford studio, and that's where we were to shoot the lake. Our call that morning was at some ungodly hour like five or six, because that's when the mist would look best over the lake (and we wouldn't have to add any phony mist to embellish the scene). Although we were supposed to start shooting at six-thirty or seven o'clock, Don Adams, our secret agent Maxwell Smart, showed up for work at noon.

He walked on the set and said, "Okay, which one of you is the director?" I was sitting in the back on my director's chair, and I raised my hand. He walked over and told me he had been playing cards all night with Hugh Hefner. "I'm ready now," he said. "Let's get going." Don acted like we were now holding him up, and he gave no apologies for his tardiness and the fact that he'd cost the production company tens of thousands of dollars.

However, he was more than the star of *Get Smart.* Don was the show's leader, and he set the tone each day. If he showed up in a good mood, it would be a nice day. If he showed up in a lousy mood, it could be a long and tedious day. He was kind of a bully in that he picked on people who couldn't fight back. He was particularly unpleasant to a female script supervisor and to his stand-in, who was his cousin. Those were givens. But with the rest of us, his attitude could change with the wind.

Once in a while, usually on a Friday afternoon, we would be shooting and Don would get a phone call on the set. When he hung up the phone, inevitably he would say he had to go to Las Vegas. This happened several times and I was told that it was because of gambling debts. He owed somebody in Vegas money, so when a headliner like Sammy Davis, Jr., canceled a show due to illness or whatever, Don had to fill in without any notice. He was at somebody's beck and call, and the arrangement apparently wasn't open to discussion.

Many people over the years have asked me about Barbara Feldon, who played Agent 99 on *Get Smart*. I'm pleased to report she was a lady from her head to her toes. Not only was she bright and professional, but also a good sport and I think the anchor of the show.

One of the other great things I remember about *Get Smart* was the actor who played the Chief, Edward Platt. He had been a character actor in movies for years and was well respected and well liked. I recall there were weeks when we couldn't get the show shot in the allotted three and a half days. So, once a month we would take an entire day and shoot several episodes' worth of the Chief's long speeches to Maxwell Smart. As tedious as this was, Platt never complained. He was a real trooper.

One of the most common questions people ask me is how sitcoms have changed over time. When I think about the way television used to be in the 1960s, I picture a time when *The Andy Griffith Show, Gomer Pyle, U.S.M.C.,* and *The Dick Van Dyke Show* were at the top of the ratings. As legend has it, CBS president Bill Paley (or perhaps it was, as rumored, Mr. Paley's wife) felt that his network shouldn't be associated with too much "cornball." As a result, many of those shows were systematically wiped out. Other less gentle shows with new faces took their place, and I think that television suffered a great loss.

Whether you were fans of those shows or not, the sitcoms that were produced during the 1960s emphasized good clean humor and values. The plots focused on things like family, relationships, and friendships. I know I probably sound like a preacher, but I see some of the violence and abusive language in entertainment today, and it makes me want to return to that sound stage where Andy Griffith played his guitar as the crew prepared for the next shot. It was a time that we will never see again in television, and that in itself is rather sad. Decency has become an entertainment crime.

As the 1960s slipped into the 1970s, television changed from a single-camera into a three-camera format. A change would take place within me as a director as well: My passion and my pace increased tenfold. Each October my heart would start to race until I found another show. I had to have one. I couldn't live without one. I was high on directing. More than any other time in my career, the 1970s would be a time of professional bingeing. The more shows I directed, the more shows I wanted to direct. I felt at the top of my game and I simply couldn't get enough of television. But something would have to give, and I was perhaps most surprised of all to find out that it was my own heart.

4.

When Love Was American Style and a Chimpanzee Had His Own Sitcom

My house in Montana is about as far away from television production as you can get, but some old habits still die hard. To this day I can't let a phone ring and not pick it up. I have friends who use answering machines routinely to screen their calls, but I'd rather die than miss a call. The minute I hear a phone ring, I think it's either one of my daughters in trouble, or my agent with a job offer. My obsession even pulls me like a magnet to my house: I can't be away from home for very long without checking my messages. I know my daughters are grown and I'm semi-retired, and a random phone call most likely won't deliver a daughter in trouble or a new job. But I'm still instinctively a dad and a director. That's just the way it is.

Despite my telephone habits, my anxiety is better than it has been in years. I haven't been upset in the longest time and it's starting to make me think that my retirement could be the best thing for me physically and mentally. For years I have been taking a prescription drug called Xanex to help alleviate my anxiety attacks, but the other day when I was talking to my daughters, I realized that I haven't had a full-blown attack in more than fifteen years. In fact, lately the pills have started to make me tired because I have nothing to be anxious about. The Xanex are probably floating around my body looking for tension and only bumping into calm walls. I've decided that I'm going to talk to my doctor about cutting down on the pills, or maybe even eliminating them altogether.

I've never been in a state where I'm not actively wrestling with or aggressively worrying about something, and it all seems so foreign to me. Recently I traveled on an airplane from New York to San Francisco with my youngest daughter, Leigh, and her toddler son, Kyle. Although Kyle was in a wonderful mood throughout the five-hour flight, his body didn't stop moving, not even for a second. Like the Energizer Bunny, Kyle wiggled, squirmed, and jiggled from the moment we took off until we landed. For a child this seemed quite normal, but he reminded me a lot of myself directing television during the early 1970s. I never stopped moving, not even for a second. I was too afraid that if I slowed down for too long, it might be my last job.

▀ ▄▄ ▄▄ ▄▄ ▄

One of the best things about television directing is that you get to work with different actors with a range of talents and temperaments. One actor with the most interesting temperamental talent whom I had the pleasure of directing was Redd Foxx. I directed him for a few years in the Norman Lear series *Sanford and Son* about father and son junk dealers, which co-starred Demond Wilson. Overall, I would have to say that I adored Redd. But the day-to-day reality was that working with Redd meant learning to work with conflict. One thing was for sure: Working with Redd was never dull.

He was a man who openly did drugs and wore spoons around his neck as a show of his allegiance to cocaine. The major battles Redd and I had were not about artistic differences, but the fact that I wouldn't do drugs with him. When I said no, he'd take it personally, as if I didn't want to be his friend. My rejection didn't slow him down, though. On show night, we had to assign the assistant director to wipe her own nose in front of Redd to remind him that there might be some white powder above his lip.

In addition to the drugs, I think part of the problem with Redd was that NBC didn't quite know what to do with him. He was enormously talented and made a lot of money for the network. At one time he was the star of the highest-rated NBC sitcom on the air, yet he was also the only comedy star in the NBC stable who didn't have his own TV variety special. I always felt that he deserved a lot more credit than he got.

All it would have taken was for somebody at NBC to run to the department store across the street, buy a cashmere sweater, and slip it into Redd's dressing room with a note that said, "Thank you. We appreciate everything that you've done." That would have meant a lot to Redd, but it never happened. The respect just wasn't there.

Some people were scared of Redd, but most of the time he was just putting on an act. He always maintained that he hated children, but I saw a different side of him when he invited my daughters and me over to his house for brunch one Sunday. Except for the fact that his house stank of marijuana, we were surprised to find Redd a wonderful cook and delightful host. He also showed us some flowers that he had planted and introduced us to his dogs, which he adored. He had about twelve dogs at the time and my little girls, who were then four and nine, had the time of their lives.

The week after we had brunch at Redd's house, we used one of his St. Bernards in *Sanford and Son*. Sadly, shortly after we shot the episode, one of his neighbors served poisoned meat to his dogs and they all died. Redd was inconsolable when he found out. He was a tremendous dog lover and I'm sure it took a long time for him to get over the loss.

In addition to his home, Redd also was host to many guests in his two connecting dressing rooms on the set of *Sanford and Son*. On show night he looked like the godfather of sitcom as people lined up outside his door waiting to pay their respects. The visitors would enter, a few at a time, and find Redd sitting in a chair, wearing only his underwear and eating his dinner. The parade included the mayor of Los Angeles, several musicians, and a steady parade of women. Redd loved the ladies. And I must say the ladies loved Redd.

As far as his work went, Redd was sometimes more like a testy child than a man. We'd call rehearsal for ten o'clock in the morning. It could be two o'clock in the afternoon before Redd came strolling in. When he did finally arrive, he might say, "I was down in the parking lot. I couldn't get in the door. It was locked. I'm not kidding." He would make up a story like a little child would. The good thing was that the show required very little rehearsal because Redd knew his character, Fred Sanford, so well. It was still frustrating, though, because we had to spend so much of our time waiting around for him.

The worst week was when he simply didn't bother to show up at all. We rehearsed Monday to Thursday by using his stand-in, and then finally Redd arrived on Friday for the show. He wasn't familiar with the staging and hadn't even looked at the script. So we quickly had some cue cards made up and tried to walk him through the scenes. Somehow we made it and were able to get a show completed. With Redd, you never knew what was going to happen. It was a crapshoot. But as filthy-mouthed and drugged-out as Redd often was, deep down I always knew that there was a lot of good in him, too.

One person who lacked a lot of good was Redd's co-star, Demond Wilson. He was one of the most evil actors I have ever worked with. Ironically, I heard that after leaving his television career behind, he became an evangelical minister. On *Sanford and Son* Demond was nothing but trouble for me and Redd. It wasn't enough that he had no respect at all for the rehearsal process, but he also used to needle Redd, increasing his feelings of paranoia and anger.

Both men carried guns. (Demond's was kept in a dramatic velvet case.) Sometimes they would get stoned and start to play with their guns. I was scared someone was going to get killed (mainly me). The guns were primarily for protection because Redd was paranoid that he was going to be attacked and Demond often fueled his anxiety. Demond could just never leave bad enough alone. If someone said something negative about Redd, Demond would walk over and twist the knife a little further into Redd's heart.

One of the reasons that Redd and I were able to work together was because I was sometimes testy, too. I even was known to throw a tantrum or two when provoked. Some people get pissed off about time or creative material, but for me it was food. On Friday night when I've finished a show, I expect to be fed. I don't think it's too much to ask. I've done my job and I expect to be rewarded with food. I'm like Pavlov's dogs when it comes to my show-night dinner.

One Friday in between the afternoon and the evening shows on *Sanford and Son*, I went down to get my dinner and was told there was no food left.

"What do you mean?" I asked the head of catering.

"I'm sorry Mr. Rafkin, but Mr. Foxx had so many guests tonight that there's nothing left," he said. "All the food is gone."

I looked around the buffet table and saw empty chafing dishes, maybe twenty of them lined up. Suddenly my hunger got the best of me. I slowly and methodically walked around the room turning the empty dishes upside down and knocking them to the floor. I tipped over one after the other, being very loud because I was so mad. Looking back on it now, I was probably being more than a little bratty, but I don't think that's the worst thing a director can be. If you're nice all the time, you'll get the reputation of being too soft. Once in awhile, I think knocking a chafing dish on the ground can earn you a little respect and, in the end, some food. Needless to say, the catering department made sure I was well fed for the rest of the series.

Even before *Sanford and Son* my career had kicked into high gear, but unfortunately my marriage to Ann had not. We had separated for a year and then got back together long enough to adopt Leigh, but we soon realized that despite the love we shared for our daughters, our marriage was over. We separated again when Leigh was a year old and Dru was six. Because of my two daughters, my separation from their mother was a miserable and unhappy time for me. I was always one of those fathers who could never go to bed without checking to see that both my girls were breathing, or going in just to kiss them one last time.

When I moved out of the house I shared with Ann and the girls, I moved into a place on La Cienega Boulevard. In those days it was called a halfway house because it was filled with men who had recently either separated or become divorced from their wives. The apartments came completely furnished, and you could move in with nothing but a toothbrush. Everything else you needed was already there.

I lived in that apartment for about a year and spent most of my time crying because I missed Leigh and Dru so much. But as much as I wanted to keep our family together, I knew that Ann and I couldn't live under the same roof. We were too immature and raw, and couldn't even pretend to be nice to each other anymore. Our custody arrangement was that I would have the girls on weekends. During that time I would change Leigh's diapers, make meals for Dru, and do the best I could.

At least once a weekend, the girls and I would have an outing. One Sunday we went to the pony rides at a place called Beverly Park. While I was putting Dru on one of the horses, I started to look around at the other people at the park. Suddenly I realized that the place was filled with divorced fathers who had their children for the weekend. It was so pathetic. I remember standing in the middle of the park, taking both of my girls' hands and trying hard not to burst into tears. This was not what I had planned for my life or the life of my daughters. This was not the way I wanted to raise my family, or the way I wanted to be a father.

I had wanted to raise my children so much better than I had been raised by my parents. But that weekend at the pony rides I realized that in my effort to please my girls, I was trying to make it like Christmas for them every weekend. It wasn't a realistic arrangement for me or for them. I sat down with Dru, because I thought she could understand (Leigh was too small), and I told her how I wanted things to be different. I said, "There's not going to be presents and some weird, wonderful place for us to go every weekend. Sometimes we might just sit in the apartment and stare at each other's faces for the whole weekend. Is that okay with you?" She said yes, and then I knew everything would be all right.

Sunday nights when I had to take the girls back to Ann were the toughest times of all. Ann and I were not on friendly terms in the beginning, so I would simply walk the girls up to the front door, kiss them goodbye, and they would disappear. I would walk back to my car and get inside. Then I'd sit there in front of the house and scream at God, cry, and carry on until I was just too exhausted to do anything but drive home and go to sleep.

▬ ▬ ▬ ▬ ▲

Ironically, just as my marriage to Ann was ending, I had started to direct a series called *Love, American Style*. Each episode featured skits on dating, romance, marriage, and even a divorce or two. Basically the series was *The Love Boat* of its time. We took stars on their way down (and in a few cases on their way up) and used them in an anthology format. The production pace on each episode was very fast, and the biggest challenge was working with an entirely new cast every week.

Each skit on *Love, American Style* ran about thirteen pages and we had to shoot those pages, and sometimes more, in one day using actors we usually had never met before (and most of the time never saw again). The task was made even more difficult because sometimes the actors came unprepared. Whether we had to use cue cards, or shoot until midnight, we did whatever we had to do to get the show on the air.

One day I was set to direct a skit with Steve Allen and Jayne Meadows. Jayne arrived on the set totally prepared, but Steve didn't know his name. He hadn't memorized a word of the script. Jayne took me aside and said, "I swear he told me before he went to bed last night that he had memorized his lines." Well, Steve hadn't. That day on the *Love* set turned out to be even longer than usual, as we gave Steve time to become more familiar with the script.

I also directed segments of *Love, American Style* that featured Ozzie and Harriet Nelson, Billy Barty, Michele Lee, Tina Louise, Cesar Romero, and Jerry Van Dyke. One of my favorite memories is of directing a skit with Mclean Stevenson before his days on the TV series *M*A*S*H*. Back then Mclean was just a day player, but he was simply a great guy to be around. He was one of the great raconteurs. When there was free time on the set, he would entertain us with the most marvelous stories about everything and anything. He was simply amusing. Later, when he moved up to starring roles, I think he just couldn't handle the pressure. Possibly the pressure is what ended up killing him.

The more episodes of *Love, American Style* I directed, the more the producers hired me to direct. Sometimes I had to shoot thirty to forty pages in two days. To give you an idea of how frantic the pace was, in feature films a director might shoot two pages a day. There I was, trying to cram in dozens of pages, so it was not surprising that things were intense on the set. Whether it was "Love and the Anniversary," "Love and the Athlete," or "Love and the Comedy Team," we shot it in a day or two and moved on to the next episode.

I directed *Love, American Style* for over a year and then was made executive producer. I decided to take the job because I thought it would give me a nice temporary break from directing. I was still living in the apartment building for divorced dads when I started to feel overloaded. In the morning sometimes I couldn't remember which show I was directing that day. I'd sit there paralyzed at the wheel of my car trying to decide if I needed to go left or right. So when the opportunity to become executive producer of *Love, American Style* came up, I took it. Each morning thereafter, I'd wake up and know immediately which direction to go.

What I didn't anticipate was that the show's executive producing job was designed for a gorilla, not a man. I thought it would offer more stability than directing, but it was completely the opposite. Where previously there had been two or three executive producers on the series, I suddenly became the only one. I was constantly consumed with editing and working with the writers. Whenever I thought I finally had things under control, I'd get a call from one of the sets about an actor who wasn't performing well.

One day it was Doug McClure who was misbehaving. The director told me that he was not prepared and was acting a little weird. This news put me in an uncomfortable position because I was friendly with Doug, and had always adored his work. I went down to the set and saw that Doug obviously had something in his system.

Whatever he was on, Doug was in another world. When he saw me he said, "You watch this rehearsal and if you don't think I'm doing my job then just go ahead and send me home." It was a fair enough offer and I took it. I watched Doug and the other actors rehearse the scene and it was more than embarrassing. It was awful. I said to Doug, "We both know that you're simply not with it today. Please go home." We replaced him immediately with another actor. I didn't have any other choice. It was my job as executive producer to make this kind of decision, and I called it like I saw it.

Later that day I was in my office when I heard a loud noise outside. Doug came bursting through the door calling me all kinds of names. He grabbed me from behind my desk and wrestled me to the floor. He was very strong and much more athletic than me. Just as suddenly as the fight had begun, however, Doug burst into tears. I put my arms around him as he wept. I suppose what happened was that when we let him go, he went home and was chastised by his wife for being fired. He just couldn't keep it all together. He was a puddle right there in my office.

The next few times when I ran into him, I could never count on what kind of mood I might find. Most of the time he was belligerent and abrasive. Then finally one day we ran into each other and he said, "I'm trying to mend some fences. Can I give you a hug?" I said, "You bettcha." And we hugged. I saw Doug one more time while having lunch at the Universal commissary. We talked like old friends. The next thing I knew, he had passed away from cancer. He was too young to go so soon.

The year I was executive producer of *Love, American Style* was very tiring, but ultimately satisfying. I met a lot of terrific people and worked with a lot of wonderful actors and actresses, but when the producers asked me to do it again the next year, I said no, thanks. I knew that it simply wasn't the right job for me. It took me away from my daughters too much, and it made me realize how much I missed directing. So, I returned to my post as director, happy to have had a taste of producing so I knew what it was all about.

With the exception of *Love, American Style,* most of the shows I directed during the 1970s were shot with several cameras, instead of one like in the 1960s. Often these multicamera shows were filmed in front of a live audience, which would supply laughter for the finished product instead of the old, dated canned or prerecorded laugh tracks. For actors, the introduction of the studio audience made filming similar to performing a stage play.

Usually we would shoot scene by scene chronologically, without any break within a scene. Sometimes, however, things could go wrong. For example, an actor might flub his or her lines. The first time an actor flubs a line, the audience loves it because it melts the ice. Many of them are on a sound stage for the first time, and their tendency is to be too quiet, even after the warm-up comic has told them to relax. So, when an actor they have adored for years forgets a line or says, "Oh, shit," the audience laughs its tension away. It puts everyone at ease, and then the show can get underway.

Sitcoms are shot on a five-day schedule. Many of the shows I directed ran on a Monday-to-Friday time table (while others worked on a Wednesday-to-Tuesday turnaround). We would get the week's script on Monday, or sometimes if we were very lucky the previous Friday night, or by messenger Saturday morning. Then Monday morning we'd start by sitting around a big table and reading the script out loud. The group would include me and the actors as well as several producers and one or two representatives from the network or studio.

I would read the stage directions out loud so the script supervisor could time the show and tell me if we were long, short, or in between. (The entertainment content of a half-hour sitcom is around twenty-one minutes. The rest is commercials and other announcements.) After we finished reading the script through at least once, the network or studio people met with me and the producers to give their notes. They usually offered specific comments about the scenes they liked and in some cases disliked.

After taking lunch we'd begin blocking out the scenes on the stage. Supposedly during lunch, whatever changes were asked for in the script would have been made by the writing staff. That's pretty optimistic, however, because the writing staff ate lunch, too. So in reality any new pages were not seen until later that night or the next day. While waiting, the cast and I might start to work on a scene that wasn't going to be changed, or the one we thought would be changed the least. On Monday, we'd rehearse until about five.

On Tuesday morning we'd come in and continue with the staging. If more than a few scenes had been heavily rewritten, we'd read the script out loud again. But for the most part we'd get up and stage all day Tuesday with a lunch break, followed by more rehearsal and a run-through at three o'clock. The first run-through was fairly rough because the actors usually still had their scripts in hand. The benefit was for the producers and writers to see what direction the actors and I had taken. Sometimes the discussions after the run-through were heated, while at other times we could just sail through. It all depended on the script and what shape it was in. If things weren't working, I'd know it and we'd try to smooth out the rough spots. I'd try and work with the actors, writers, producers, and crew to create something that we could all be proud of.

On Wednesday rehearsing would continue, incorporating any changes that may have been made as the result of Tuesday's run-through. Wednesday run-throughs would be much better, even though for the most part the actors had still not memorized their lines. Wednesday night, I'd take my script home and start marking it with the shots I wanted to see.

Thursday was camera blocking day. The crew included cameramen, assistants, operators, lighting people, grips, and dolly pushers. It's a good group and if you get a crew that's happy, it makes the week all the better. I've observed that most of the crew members are great to work with because they are so happy to be employed. Most have to work at least two different shows because it has become only a six-month business for them. They may shoot for one show on Friday night and then another on Tuesday night. When I met with the crew on Thursday, I'd tell them what I wanted for each shot.

Friday we'd come in around noon. The actors would go to makeup and we'd come back and rehearse each scene at least twice. Sometimes we would do another run-through if the producers wanted to do some last-minute tinkering. If not, we'd break after rehearsal and get ready to shoot the show twice, in front of an audience both times. The first show was at 3:30 P.M. Then we'd break for a light dinner and come back and do the second show at 7:30 P.M. The afternoon audience was usually made up of old people, homeless folks, and generally anyone who needed to get in from the cold. The evening performance was viewed by a higher caliber of fan, usually by people who had written in and waited weeks for tickets.

That's generally a week in the life of a multicamera sitcom.

The method really came to the forefront of production with *I Love Lucy*. Although some shows even as early as the 1950s used the technique, Desi Arnaz brought it to a level of sophistication it never had before. Even though I loved working this way, I would get flop sweat before every show night. I used to think that eventually my nervousness would disappear, but Sheldon Leonard cautioned me against that. He said that when your nerves disappear, it's time to get out of the business. He was probably right. Fear is a great motivator.

When I'd get into my car to drive home after shooting a show Friday night that went well, I felt completely exhilarated. But if I had just finished directing a show I was not completely happy with, I could console myself by imagining the sound of a cash register ringing. At least for a little while I could rationalize my unhappiness away with the fact that the pay was good. But I liked it the other way, when the show worked well, the audience liked it, the actors were pleased, and I felt I'd done my best work.

Sometimes there were episodes I was not proud of. Other times entire series disappointed me, and as much as I try to forget, failures follow me around. I lecture at universities to students interested in pursing careers in television and directing. Most recently, I've been to Northwestern University (where my daughter Dru graduated from) and Syracuse (my alma mater). I usually stay on campus for a few days or a week, meeting with the students. I used to give formal speeches, but after a while I got tired of hearing my own voice. Now I send ahead a script (from maybe *Coach* or *Murphy Brown*) and tell the students to plot out and cast the episode. When I arrive on campus I take them through a mock shooting week.

Most of the time I am very pleased with how bright the kids are and how well they have done their homework when it comes to my career. They pretty much know all the shows I've done. But I wasn't as pleased with the students' knowledge of my credits the day a boy at Northwestern raised his hand. He said, "Mr. Rafkin, you're an Emmy winner. What were you thinking when you decided to direct *Me and the Chimp?*" My answer was that I was thinking like a divorced dad with two small daughters who wanted to make money, rather than an artist who easily would have run the other way when handed a script that starred a chimpanzee.

I had been producing *Love, American Style,* when Tom Tennenbaum, then vice president of programming for Paramount TV, called me into his office. He explained that he had an exciting new series starring Ted Bessell, who had been so charming on *That Girl* as Don Hollinger (even though the audience spent more time looking at Marlo's face and the back of Ted's head). The new series was called *Me and the Chimp.* The concept was about a southern California dentist and his family, who adopt a chimpanzee named Buttons. Each week the chimp would get the family into some kind of trouble, and it would usually rest on the dad's shoulders to get them out.

Tom is a great salesman, and I bought his pitch hook, line, and sinker. He had me convinced that people across America were going to give up dogs as pets and buy chimps instead. I couldn't wait to be a part of the new trend as the director of the sitcom. That day I went out of his office pumped up as if Vince Lombardi had just given me the greatest pep talk of all time. And, as if agreeing to direct the series wasn't bad enough, I also took a cut in salary to become the show's producer. *Me and the Chimp* would prove to be one of the worst shows ever on television, and one of the most unpleasant experiences of my life.

At the time of the show, I was dating an Italian woman. When things on the set of *Me and the Chimp* became bad, she gave me a novena card. Every morning before work I would sit in my car in the studio parking lot with the card and pray to get through the day. Ted Bessell, whom I had enjoyed working with on *That Girl* because he was so funny and talented, had become my worst nightmare. As the star of his own series, he had taken a 180-degree turn in the wrong direction.

The work was embarrassing to both of us, and it provoked nothing but conflict. One day Ted became so angry at me that the cinematographer had to step between us before things became violent. I didn't mind the interference, because when you're my size you don't win many fights. At the time I felt that Ted and I didn't get along because we were so different from one another. But looking back, I think that we were really very similar. We were both people who found it difficult to paste smiles on our faces when we knew we were in the dumps. Directing *Me and the Chimp* was about as far as I have ever sunk. We were all thankful that the series was off the air after only one season.

⬤▬▬▬▬◣

While *Me and the Chimp* is one of my most unpleasant memories, the pilot I directed for another 1970s series is one of my fondest. A pilot is a presentation done for a network to see if they want to make a series of the concept for the following season. The first pilot I ever directed was *The Courtship of Eddie's Father* for Jimmy Komack, a former night-club comedian turned actor and then television producer. I first saw Jimmy perform as the catcher in *Damn Yankees* on Broadway and had a great regard for him ever since.

My pay to direct the pilot for *The Courtship of Eddie's Father* for the 1969–70 season was $13,000. In the 1990s I would get somewhere over $100,000 for a single pilot episode. Today there are other directors who certainly take home more than I do, like Jim Burrows, whose track record is lined with shows like *Friends, Cheers,* and *Third Rock from the Sun.* Basically, Burrows gets first crack at all the NBC pilots and money to match.

When I first met with Jimmy Komack to talk about *The Courtship of Eddie's Father,* he told me that the star was Bill Bixby, whom I had worked with on *My Favorite Martian.* The chance to work with Bill again made me feel comfortable about the project, although Bill was a person I found it difficult to connect with. Looking back I think that like Ted Bessell, Bill and I were similar in many ways. Bill was as involved and addicted to his acting career as I was to directing. At times our dedication got in the way of our relationship.

Before directing the pilot, I went to Jimmy's house to meet with Bill and the actor set to play his TV son, Brandon Cruz. When I arrived, Brandon (then about seven years old) was in the pool with Bill. I sat for a few minutes watching the two of them as they splashed around, and it gave me great confidence in the pilot. I knew that even if nothing else went right, their relationship worked. There was a chemistry between them that would give credibility to their roles as the widower and his young son.

I loved directing the pilot, particularly because we took some chances that paid off. We came up with a great idea for the opening titles (and many other sequences within the series) to use a long lens so the figures of Eddie and Tom Corbett would appear quite small on screen. Over the shots we laced in some dialogue voice-over: Why is the sky blue? Why did God take Mommy away? And other philosophical questions from child to parent. Bill would answer like a thoughtful dad. The segments were successful because the more we did them, the more it not only brought the characters together, but Bill and Brandon as well.

Sometimes I would use Bill's close relationship with Brandon to help me direct the boy. If I wanted Brandon to do some action in a scene, I might mention it to Bill first and then have him explain the piece of direction. Brandon seemed to treasure his relationship with Bill because it was so idealistic compared to his own reportedly dysfunctional real-life family.

ABC bought the pilot for *The Courtship of Eddie's Father* immediately. Considering that this was the first pilot I had ever directed, I was euphoric. I felt like I had finally launched something of my own without having to work in the shadow of a director who had come before me. Unfortunately, I never did another episode of the show. Jimmy refused to pay me over scale to continue as the director, and even in those days, I wasn't about to work for scale (which is the lowest amount a director could legally be paid).

It was time for me once again to move on to another series. I had to keep moving. Standing still was not an option.

Room 222 was a schoolroom drama about an integrated big-city high school. I directed episodes of the show, which was blessed with a wonderful writing staff and a fine cast of actors including Lloyd Haynes, Denise Nicholas, Michael Constantine, and Karen Valentine. I'll never

forget one particular episode of the show when we used a choir of real-life students from one of the inner city schools in Los Angeles. The students were as thrilled to be on the set as we were to have them. Their voices were magnificent, and the kids themselves were just marvelous to be around.

The amazing thing about the choir was the looks on their faces. You could tell from their eyes that they knew they were in a place they had never imagined they would be. They never expected to end up on a sound stage with actors on television, but there they were singing on the tube. Their performance in the episode was outstanding, which made it even more difficult for all of us when it was time to say goodbye. It wasn't like I had gotten to know any of them very well, but when we finished the last shot it was emotional for me. They were going back to a place that I imagined wasn't nearly as intriguing and as uplifting as the couple of days they had spent on the set of *Room 222*. And I thought that was sad. I still do.

After the school choir, I worked with music on a series called *The Partridge Family*. I directed a few episodes during the time when David Cassidy was as hot as could be. Magazine covers. Lunch boxes. T-shirts. He was everywhere. I haven't seen him since, but when we worked together, I thought he was one hell of a young man. I admired him, but at the same time felt a sense of sadness for him because he was so clearly overwhelmed by his fame. He was deluged by people wanting to get a piece of him. Even though he seemed to handle it well, it couldn't have been easy.

In every episode of *The Partridge Family* we had to do a few musical numbers, and that always took a long time. We prerecorded all the music, though, which gave us the leisure to play around with the songs and staging when it came time to shoot. The producers and David's popularity among teenagers dictated that he be the star of the series. Unfortunately this billing left little to do for the supporting cast, which included Susan Dey, Danny Bonaduce, and David's real-life stepmom, Shirley Jones.

Shirley Jones, who starred in many Rodgers and Hammerstein musicals on Broadway before joining *The Partridge Family*, is a lady you could instantly fall in love with. She's just nice. That's that. Nice in the way that Shelley Fabares is nice. Nice in the way most human beings should be nice but truly are not.

When I say the word "nice" and the word "sitcom" two other words immediately come to mind: Mary Richards. It's probably not a big surprise to anyone who watched *The Mary Tyler Moore Show* regularly, that Mary was as polite and professional in front of the camera as she was behind the scenes.

Although I enjoyed working with her, she seemed to act from behind a shield of thick plastic. Like her former co-star Dick Van Dyke, she would be great with an audience, while at the same time she didn't give anything of herself backstage. First and foremost Mary was a businesswoman and she ran her series beautifully. She was the boss, and although you weren't always wedded to doing things exactly her way, you never forgot for a second that she was in charge.

While the happiest moments in my life were unquestionably the births of my two daughters, followed by the birth of my grandson, I must say with a certain amount of ego that being nominated for an Emmy award for directing *The Mary Tyler Moore Show* still means a lot to me. The nomination represents an accomplishment that nobody can ever take away.

I have been nominated for an Emmy award four times for directing a television series. The first was for an episode of *The Mary Tyler Moore Show* called "Support Your Local Mother," which introduced Nancy Walker to the series as Rhoda (Valerie Harper) Morgenstern's mother. I lost that time to a friend and wonderful sitcom director named Jay Sandrich. Jay won that night for an episode of *The Mary Tyler Moore Show* he had directed.

I was sitting next to Ed Asner, who played Lou Grant on *The Mary Tyler Moore Show,* when they announced Jay as the winner. Ed put his hand on my arm, squeezed it and said, "You know there'll be other times." Later Jay came by and said, "I just want you to know that the only reason I won was because I directed more episodes than you." How could I be disappointed when everyone was being so supportive?

(Luckily I would later be nominated for three more Emmys and take one home for an episode of *One Day at a Time*.)

Another classic 1970s sitcom I directed was *The Odd Couple* starring Jack Klugman as Oscar Madison and Tony Randall as Felix Unger. When I started with the show, it was still shot using a single camera. Eventually the show changed over to a multicamera format. Whether we had one camera or three or four, however, my memories are that Tony Randall was a pain in the ass. For example, if he smelled cigarette smoke on the stage (and this was way before smoking was banned on stages), he started yelling, "The person who is smoking is now fired." He could be snide, but once I called him on it, we could get down to the business of doing the show.

Jack Klugman was a joy to work with and a lot of fun. I was living in Malibu at the time and so was he. I would walk by his condo or run into him on the beach and he was always delightful. *The Odd Couple* was an extremely tough show to direct because Jack and Tony were very opinionated about how they wanted the show to be. We all put up with a lot from them, especially Tony, because we knew that one thing was for sure: Jack and Tony were more than funny as Oscar and Felix. They were hands-down marvelous in their roles. To get marvelous, you can put up with a lot.

■ ▰ ▰ ▰ ▰

During my marriage to Ann I had been a faithful husband, although I had flirted with a stunt woman I ran into from time to time. The night I moved out of the house, one of the first things I did was pick up the phone and call that stunt woman. I said, "I'm free." Her response was "Great, I'll be right over." She came to the apartment where I was staying and brought along a marijuana joint.

I had never smoked pot before and that night we made love, as far as I can remember, at least six times. Something like that has never happened to me since. I used to think that my virility was because of the marijuana. But looking back, I think you could have given me bubblegum and it would have been just as much of an aphrodisiac. I was just excited about having finally called an end to my marriage, and about having the chance to finally be alone with the stunt woman I had been flirting with for so long. I've smoked a couple of joints since then, perhaps twenty-five years ago, and they never had the same potency.

The early 1970s not only opened the door for me to act on my flirtations, but also for me to continue to feed my insatiable appetite for television directing. In addition to *Sanford and Son, Love, American Style*, and the others I've mentioned, I also directed episodes of *The Governor & J. J., Valentine's Day, Nanny and the Professor, The Tim Conway Show, Bridget Loves Bernie, Another April*, and *Paul Sand in Friends and Lovers*. The more the merrier. I probably would have directed two shows at once if they had let me.

There is no question that I was addicted to the stuff by now. I was addicted in the sense that television had now become my identity. I had to have it. I had to work. I had to know every May or June what my shows were for the coming season. I decided that if everything wasn't perfect in my personal life, I would simply direct more television shows. Like an addict goes for a fix, or an alcoholic goes for the booze, I went for television. I knew that no matter how bad the weekend had been, I had my Monday morning rehearsal to look forward to. The sound stage was my turf and the sitcom was my drug of choice.

The solid ground of my turf began to falter one day in 1975. I was directing a Don Knotts movie called *How to Frame a Fig*. I was handling the shoot pretty well until the morning I ate the bacon and egg sandwich. I had never been a big breakfast eater, but for some reason that morning I indulged myself. I had seen grips and other crew members returning from the catering truck eating greasy breakfast combinations with onions and peppers. I just had to try something greasy too.

Shortly after I ate the sandwich, I felt a little strange. I thought it was simply indigestion because I wasn't used to eating such heavy food. I had indigestion all day. A nurse on the set gave me Pepto Bismol℗, and then Alka Seltzer℗, but nothing worked. I just couldn't get rid of that queasy feeling. What I soon found out was that at forty-seven years old, I was having a heart attack.

5.

Mending My Heart while Directing
*M*A*S*H* and Bob Newhart

In our family my sister Claire was the oldest and she was always considered the family's jewel. My father worked long and hard to get her married. He sent her on cruises and to resorts in the mountains, all in an orchestrated effort to find her a husband. I was starting to feel sorry for her (and a little embarrassed) until she met Danny Feldstein. He was a welcomed addition to our family because, unlike the rest of us, he never had anything but a smile on his face. If I could have created the perfect brother-in-law, it would have been Danny.

He was the kind of person who didn't let anything get to him. My father, in his traditional fashion, could be rude to Danny. He would say, "Danny, why don't you get your hair cut?" or "Danny, how can you wear that suit?" But no matter what my father said, Danny would simply let it roll off him. He sometimes would just smile right back at my father, which infuriated Dad. My sister, from what I saw, had the perfect marriage until one Sunday morning. Danny and Claire were in bed doing the *New York Times* crossword puzzle when she got up to get him some orange juice. When she came back from the kitchen with the juice, Danny was dead. He had died of a heart attack at thirty-eight years old.

News of Danny's death reached me by phone in California. When my brother, David, called and said "Danny" had died I thought he said "Daddy," resulting in about ten minutes of confusion on the phone. It was bizarre. When I finally realized it was my brother-in-law who had died, I told my secretary to get me a plane ticket to New York.

She said, "Don't you mean two?"

I was married to Ann at the time but it was clear that my subconscious already knew we were never meant to be a couple. "No," I said. "One ticket will be fine."

I was told that my father cried when he heard Danny died, and that he continued to cry for days after that. He would sit in his office and swivel around to look out over Fifth Avenue and sob. Eleven weeks later my father woke up in the middle of the night and got out of bed. My mother thought he was going to the bathroom. Suddenly he stopped short and fell down. He suffered a cerebral hemorrhage and died instantly. I've often thought it was the anger and anxiety that killed him. It seemed the best explanation for my father's sudden death at sixty.

My father was five-foot-three-inches tall and had a slim build, except for his abdomen. From the side it looked like he had two pillows strapped onto the front of his body. His tummy was distended, the result of the rich food and lack of exercise that was typical in those days. I am built exactly the same way as my father, except that so far I've managed to avoid strapping on the two pillows.

Because of the way my father died, I was not entirely surprised when I found out I was having a heart attack on the set of the Don Knotts movie in 1970. The men in my life had a way of dying young. On the set, producer Ed Montagne came over to me and said, "You don't look so good." I tried to cover up what was happening. I said, "It's nothing. Just a little indigestion." Toward the end of the day, Ed called for a limousine to take me to the hospital. I managed to shoot one more scene before they practically had to push me into the car. As the limo pulled away from the location, I got the eerie feeling that I was driving to my own funeral. But I was too busy thinking about my next shot to let it sink in.

When I used to picture what having a heart attack was like, I certainly didn't imagine what happened to me. It didn't knock me off my feet, or take my breath away. It wasn't the kind of pain that you read about in *Reader's Digest*, with bands of steel and fire wrapped around your chest. It didn't feel extraordinary, but rather mimicked ordinary indigestion.

When I arrived at the hospital, Dr. Joseph Marx gave me an EKG and a battery of other tests. After reviewing the test results, he said, "Your heart looks fine. Go home and rest. Come back tomorrow."

I went back the next day. He took another EKG and his tone changed.

"You had a heart attack," he said.

"When? In the middle of the night? This morning?" I asked.

"Yesterday."

"How could I have a heart attack and not know it?"

"It was a mild one, but still a heart attack," he said.

Of course when a doctor delivers that kind of news to you, it's like being handed a second chance at your life. You almost died, but didn't, so now shape up or you'll ship out next time. From the moment I was given the news in 1970, I started taking better care of myself. There were two things that immediately improved my health: I stopped smoking and I got divorced. I remember a shrink I was seeing at the time said that if I didn't get a divorce soon, the tension from my marriage was going to kill me. There were certain things that I was willing to do to ensure my health. Getting a divorce, eating better, and exercising more were viable options. Cutting back on directing was not. That price was too high to pay.

▀ ▄▀ ▄▀ ▄▀ ▄

It wasn't just the directing part of my job that I loved. It also was the perks. I loved the perks. I loved saying I was a television director and watching people's eyes light up in response. I loved the money. I relished driving through the studio gates and pulling up to a parking spot that had my name stenciled on it. I liked walking on the stage and having fifty questions thrown my way and answering them to the best of my ability. I guess the bottom line was that I loved the power. I was well suited to being in charge. The set was my terrain.

When things at work were going my way, I felt like a king. I felt really good inside. But by the same token, when things were going badly, it could eat me up inside. If a producer was looking over my shoulder in a disapproving manner, I knew he didn't like what he was seeing and it would make my stomach drop out. Or if I came to work in the morning and an actor didn't say hello to me, I would start to worry that something was wrong. If an actor clearly didn't want to be there, then it was awful for me to be there, too.

Again, part of the way I got through the rough times was by thinking about the money. The payment for a sitcom director ranges greatly from show to show. Today scale (the lowest a member of the Directors Guild of America can be paid) is around $17,000 per episode. For the last five years of my career during the early 1990s, I was getting $35,000 an episode. If you estimate that a director can do about twenty shows a season, it's a pretty great living. What makes it even better are the residuals, money received when shows are aired in reruns through syndication. The first time a show is rerun on a network, a director's share of a show like *Coach* is something like $8,000. A director's check diminishes with each rerun, but it never gets below $400 or $500. It's impressive no matter how you slice up the pie.

For me the bells and whistles that came with directing also were addictive. Instead of working on building healthy relationships outside of work, I would direct *M*A*S*H*, or *The Dick Van Dyke Show*, or *The Mary Tyler Moore Show*. That's what kept me going. There wasn't much else happening in my life apart from my children. So the fact that I could call myself a successful director was what gave me comfort. I would say to myself, "Thank God, you are at least that."

The mid-1970s was a good time, and a very busy one for me. I continued to direct episodes of *Sanford and Son*, and added *That's My Mama* with Clifton Davis, *The Girl with Something Extra* with Sally Field, *Bewitched* with Elizabeth Montgomery. *The Cop and the Kid* with Charles Durning, *Lotsa Luck* with Dom DeLuise, *Here We Go Again* with Larry Hagman, and *The New Dick Van Dyke Show* to name just a few. Some were hits and some were flops, but the stars were getting bigger and better and so was my directing résumé.

I also directed a series in 1976 that probably nobody saw called *The Nancy Walker Show*. Norman Lear produced the series, which centered around Nancy's job as a Hollywood talent agent and co-starred Bill Daniels as her husband. Even though the show wasn't a hit, Nancy was pure joy to work with. Unfortunately, sometimes shows you love with talented people don't make it for one reason or another.

By the time I worked with her, Nancy had already done all there was to do in show business. It wasn't a surprise to hear that she was raised around vaudeville and the nightclub circuit, where her father worked as a comic. Nancy inherited her father's love for performing, and she was a wonderful lady and a privilege to direct. (I later would direct her again in *Rhoda*, where she played Valerie Harper's mother, Ida Morgenstern.)

A few weeks after *The Nancy Walker Show* was canceled in mid-season, Nancy showed up as the star of a Garry Marshall series called *Blansky's Beauties*, which I directed. She played the den mother to a group of Las Vegas showgirls. I originally had directed another Garry Marshall pilot called *Legs*, which also was about a group of Vegas showgirls, but never sold. When Nancy came on board, they changed the name of the series to *Blansky's Beauties* and dubbed her Nancy Blansky. But sadly, neither a name change nor Nancy's talent could save the sitcom, which was canceled after only thirteen episodes.

One series that not only made it, but made it big time was *The Bob Newhart Show*. I directed the series for several seasons and would have to say that Newhart was probably the most "normal" star of a sitcom I have ever directed. He was a man who had his career and family life perfectly in balance. He had been married to the same woman, Ginny, for ever and ever, and had, I think, three children at the time. No matter what, he was able to maintain a low-key mood about everything. There have been many high-anxiety, stress-riddled shows that I've directed over the years, but *Newhart* was the exact opposite.

In the series Bob played a psychologist who had a school-teacher wife named Emily (Suzanne Pleshette), a receptionist he shared with a dentist (Peter Bonerz), and a next-door neighbor (Bill Daily) who made frequent unannounced visits. The supporting cast was filled with quirky, talented comedians like Marcia Wallace, who played the receptionist, and Jack Riley, who appeared as one of Bob's regular patients.

As far as our routine went, Suzanne would rehearse whenever I wanted to, but Bob preferred to rehearse each scene only twice a day. Working with Bob was different for me because he wasn't a trained actor. I remember one time I was giving him a piece of direction and he seemed uncomfortable about it. Suddenly he walked over to a phone on the wall of the set.

"Do you see that?" asked Bob pointing to the phone.

"Yes," I said.

"That's what I do."

"What?"

"I pick up the phone and I do funny monologues," he said. "That's it."

He was referring to his hit comedy album in which he did a series of telephone monologues. I guess what he was trying to say was, "Don't try and stretch me or make me what I'm not." There was no doubt that he was wonderful on television, but he was a man who clearly knew his acting limitations. I understood his message and from then on I respected his talent the way it was. I didn't fuss, but instead left well enough alone. By show night he was usually right on track anyway.

One of my favorite people on the series was Suzanne Pleshette. She had a mouth like a sailor, but on the second day of each week she had every line of her script memorized. At the time of the show, she and a friend were partners in a firm that designed custom-made bedroom linens and accessories. If she wasn't in a scene, she'd be sitting at the actors' table sketching designs for sheets and pillow cases.

Suzanne was the first person I ever knew who was hypoglycemic. A lot of people claim they can have a bad reaction to sugar, but I witnessed Suzanne's up-close on the set. One afternoon she hadn't eaten any protein and she started to turn gray. I watched as her eyes started to roll up into her forehead right before she fainted. It was incredibly scary and not something you want to see twice.

I remember the day I found out I, too, was hypoglycemic. It was several years after *The Bob Newhart Show,* when I was working with producer Garry Marshall directing *Laverne & Shirley.* I went into Garry's office and we were discussing the tension on the set. As we were talking, I was fishing miniature chocolate bars out of a giant brandy snifter on Garry's desk and eating them one after the other. At the end of our conversation, I grabbed my chest and thought I was having a heart attack. With my heart racing, I immediately went to the hospital, but by the time I got there my symptoms had disappeared. That's when a nurse told me my heart was fine but that I was hypoglycemic. My days of bingeing on chocolate bars, miniature or otherwise, were over.

Aside from Suzanne's occasional fainting spells, the set of *The Bob Newhart Show* had the casual, festive feeling of a dinner party. Unfortunately a dinner party atmosphere isn't always the most conducive for shooting a sitcom. Some nights when we'd be on stage I could hear the click of dice backstage. It was Suzanne's husband, Tom Gallagher, and Bob's wife, Ginny, playing backgammon while waiting for their mates to finish work. I would ask the assistant director to tell them to be quiet. I felt that if I could hear the click of the dice, so could the actors who would be distracted. The assistant director's warning didn't do any good; the game went on every show night without fail.

In my professional life, there were some games I was good at, and some I was not. There was one incident that happened during *The Bob Newhart Show* that I didn't handle as well as I should have. It occurred the day after I took an afternoon off to finalize my divorce from Ann. During the time I was away from the set, the producers brought in director Jay Sandrich to rehearse with the cast. I took care of my divorce and returned to work the next day as planned. Everything seem to go smoothly.

The next week when I got my paycheck I was startled to see that the producers had deducted an afternoon's pay from my salary. I thought the deduction was petty and totally unnecessary. I didn't punch a time clock. I was a director who worked long hours and expected to be paid by the episode, not the minute. I stormed in to see the show's producers, David Davis and Lorenzo Music. They stood and listened to me rant and rave for several minutes. After I was done, David spoke. "You oughta learn to pick your fights," he said simply.

He was right. There I was screaming like a crazy man about something that deep down wasn't all that important to me. I was mad, but not about a noble subject I felt righteous about. The incident would prove to be typical of my experience with arguments. I usually entered into them because I was driven by a desire to prove without a doubt that I was the one who was right. But in the end, being right didn't mean much to me. Sometimes I just went too far. It would take a long time before I could let the little things go instead of pouncing on them just for the sake of a good pounce.

The Bob Newhart Show clearly had all the right ingredients, but there were other shows that never jelled. *A Year at the Top* was one of those. Norman Lear produced the series that starred Greg Evigan and Paul Shaffer (now of *The David Letterman Show*) as young rock musicians tempted to sell their souls to the Devil in exchange for a taste of fame. The series was difficult to do and despite our hard work, it never paid off. *A Year at the Top* hit rock bottom and was off the air within a season.

Although the show was not a success, it allowed me the chance to direct one of my long-time idols, Mickey Rooney, who appeared one week as a guest star. Unfortunately, the week I spent directing my idol was one of the longest weeks of my life. Mickey is a dear, talented man (and an episode of *The Twilight Zone* in which he plays a jockey is one of my favorites). The problem with Mickey, however, is not his acting. It's his mouth. When the cameras aren't rolling, it doesn't stop talking.

In those days Mickey was an inveterate horse gambler and he would come to work early to lay his bets down or phone his handicappers. He was always talking to somebody at the wrong time. If I was staging a scene with Greg that Mickey wasn't in, he would be standing right behind me chattering away. Finally one day I had enough and I blurted out, "Mickey, I'm working with Greg now. When I'm finished

I'm going to give you my full attention, but right now I must have this conversation with Greg." Later I regretted the outburst, but at the time I didn't know what else to do. He simply wouldn't let up.

Directors need agents to get them work, and we get work in much the same way actors do. Our agents do their best to get our names around town and submit us for shows, pilots, and other projects. When I moved to Los Angeles to direct *The Verdict Is Yours*, I didn't have an agent. Once I got settled, I became associated with a Hollywood agency called Frank Cooper and Associates. Cooper was a well-respected, old time agent and a very nice gentleman. I stayed with him for a couple of years until politically it seemed opportune for me to move to a bigger agency.

I decided to sign with William Morris because they represented most of the players on the shows I was directing for Danny Thomas and Sheldon Leonard, including the two producers themselves. After a while, however, I began to regret moving to such a large agency. It wasn't that they were doing anything wrong, it was just that I felt lost in the crowd. So I made the move to another agency called Contemporary Korman, which was run by Ronnie Leif and Tom Korman.

Tom came from the same community on Long Island that I did. He was younger than I, and a friend of my brother's, but I knew him pretty well too. My day-to-day dealings, though, were with Ronnie and the agents underneath him. In the beginning my relationship with Contemporary Korman was terrific. They were like working with a group of old time booking agents. We would sit down with my calendar. They would ask me what dates I had available and they'd fill them in.

During the mid-1970s, I directed forty shows in one year. It's almost impossible to direct so many shows now, but in those days you could work as hard as you wanted, and the work was there. Also back then a single sitcom season could include as many as forty episodes a year. Today as few as twenty-two episodes make up the season on a hit show. So, it was during my time with Contemporary Korman that I had my most prolific year as a sitcom director.

Ronnie was selling me as fast as a vaudeville act. It was wonderful on the one hand because I made a lot of money, but not so wonderful on the other hand because the emphasis was on speed rather than career advancement and enhancement. He was able to get me the Don Knotts movies to direct for Universal, but I was never able to turn those projects into a movie directing career.

My contract with Contemporary Korman was up every three years, and every three years I swore to my wife that I was going to leave the agency. Yet, every three years I would return from my meeting with Ronnie having signed on again. Ronnie would inevitably lay a load of guilt on me and I would quickly back down. It wasn't that he was trying to intimidate me; it was just that I was so easily intimidated.

Finally one year came around and I was determined to make my move. By this time Ann and I were divorced. I remember this because I was driving my post-divorce Rolls Royce, a car that looked beautiful but broke down often. I arranged to meet with Ronnie at a chic restaurant called Jimmy's in Beverly Hills. Ronnie thought we were having dinner to celebrate my re-signing, but in my heart I knew it was time for me to leave the agency.

I decided that instead of telling him at the restaurant, I would tell him before dinner when we met at his house. When I arrived we had a cocktail together, but I didn't say anything. I waited and waited, but didn't find the right opening to tell him. Then he suggested that I re-sign my contract before we went to dinner. This was my chance. I mustered up all the courage I had and told him I had decided not to re-sign.

He was shocked. His second wife, a fiery woman from Latin America, overheard me and she was pissed. Suddenly the entire house was filled with an edgy attitude from wall to wall. I had to get out of there quickly. I mumbled a few things (apologies, explanations, and other ramblings) and bolted out of the house. Once outside I got into my Rolls Royce and, of course, the damned car wouldn't start. There I was in the middle of residential Beverly Hills without a phone booth for miles. I had no choice but to go back into the house and ask to call a tow truck. Either I called or Ronnie called, I can't remember. But I know that I waited for the truck outside.

After leaving Ronnie, I went with Bernie Brillstein at the Brillstein-

Grey agency, where I remain today. Bernie has been a personal manager forever, and is considered one of the power house figures in the entertainment industry. He also is one of the all-time great characters in show business. He started out, like me, as an office boy at William Morris. Then he worked his way up to agent and eventually personal manager.

Bernie has been in the business so long he knows it better than anybody. I used to call up from the set and say things like, "I hate it here," or "I'm not being treated well," or "The acting stinks and the writing is worse." Bernie would say, "It's not going to be any better anywhere else. It's a job." That's just the way Bernie was, and I admired him a great deal. Today I'm handled personally at Brillstein-Grey by agent Sandy Wernick, who has just done a magnificent job for me. Sandy has never let me down and is one of the best negotiators in the business.

▼ ▬ ▬ ▬ ◢

Some stories come back to me when I remember the kind of car I was driving at the time. I was driving the Rolls Royce when I got a call from my mother about her Oldsmobile. My mother, who had moved to California, didn't drive very much then and didn't go on the freeways at all. Considering that Los Angeles is basically one giant freeway, her driving possibilities were limited. Driving also had begun to frighten my mother, who then was in her seventies. She called me one day and said that although her Oldsmobile only had about 12,000 miles on it, she was finished with it. She didn't want to drive any more.

I supported her decision. It made sense. If she didn't enjoy driving, why do it? Most of the places she wanted to go, like to her card games, were close enough to walk to anyway. Then she got to the real point of her call.

"I've noticed you've been having a lot of trouble with your car," she said.

"The Rolls Royce?" I said. "Yes. It's so unpredictable. I never know if it's going to start or if I'll have to take a cab to the studio."

"Would you like my car?" she asked.

"Really?"

"Sure."

"Mom, that's the sweetest thing. I'd love it. It would just make my life so much easier," I said. "In the morning if the Rolls doesn't start, then I'll just take the Olds."

"The blue book price is $300," she said, very matter-of-factly.

I didn't know what to say. I was shocked. I thought my mother was going to give me her car, but she had plans to sell it to me all along. I tried to cover my surprise by going along with her.

"How much do you want for it?" I asked.

"Would I charge you more than the blue book?" she said.

"I'll have Gelfand send you a check for $300 then."

Ironically, some months later I drove the Oldsmobile into the Rolls Royce service station to see how the latest repairs on my car were coming. While I was waiting, one of the mechanics came over to admire the Oldsmobile.

"Mr. Rafkin," he asked, "would you be interested in selling that Oldsmobile? It would be just perfect for me and my family. I'll give you $500 for it."

I'd never made money on anything outside of show business in my life before this, and here I was with the chance to make $200 on a car my mother sold me. So, I decided to dump the Olds. It was a nice profit no matter how you looked at it.

When people look at the list of shows I've directed over the years, they are most impressed by *M*A*S*H*. I agree because it's probably one of the best sitcoms that has ever come out of this business.

It was a single-camera series and we were always on location shooting a combination of interior and exterior scenes. In the mornings we'd arrive at the location and it would be freezing so we'd put on extra clothes. By the afternoon we'd all be overheated and start peeling off the layers. But despite the range in temperature and the physical demands placed on everyone, *M*A*S*H* was a series in which everything clicked.

The series had so many things going for it, not the least of which was a first-rate group of actors. Two of the people I loved working with the most were Loretta Swit (who played Margaret "Hot Lips" Houlihan) and Jamie Farr (who was hilarious as Corporal Maxwell Klinger).

Farr's character dressed in women's clothing in an attempt to get himself discharged from the army for being mentally unfit. It was hard not to have fun with a character like that.

Jamie was originally from Toledo, Ohio. More than any other actor on the series, he was sincerely grateful for the success of M*A*S*H and devoured everything about it. He gave his all to the series, every day and in every scene. Loretta did the same. She was one of those actresses who is in love with acting. I remember how tickled she got in some of the scenes with her screen boyfriend, Major Frank Burns (played by Larry Linville). One time Frank sent Hot Lips a present wrapped in a frilly way. Loretta opened it up to find a whip inside. She took out the whip and orgasmically started snapping it around. We did the scene several times and with each take I laughed harder and harder.

Loretta also shared Jamie's appreciation for the series. They filled their characters with everything they had, and at the end of the day there was nothing left to ask for. It's a director's dream to work with actors who give so freely and so abundantly. Loretta and Jamie represented what I love in actors. Don't send me any actor who's there to do me a favor. I want an actor who's thrilled to be there.

I directed M*A*S*H after McLean Stevenson and Wayne Rogers left and Harry Morgan and Mike Farrell joined the cast. As Colonel Sherman Potter, Harry Morgan was solid as a rock. I'll always remember one scene in which the power of his acting filled a room. In the episode Colonel Potter recalled how he and a bunch of buddies from World War I had bought a bottle of brandy and pledged that the last one alive would drink a toast to the others. Potter turned out to be the last one alive. In one scene we see him drink the brandy and give a toast to his fallen buddies. To watch Harry do that monologue was to watch an actor well up from his toes to his nose. It was wonderful.

Directing Mike Farrell on M*A*S*H gave me the opportunity to watch an actor turn what could have been a thankless role into something impressive. I've also gotten to know Mike personally over the years through his marriage to my friend, actress Shelley Fabares. If there was ever a match made in heaven, it was Mike and Shelley's. They also are two of the nicest people who often do good deeds without feeling compelled to shout about it from the roof tops.

As a director on M*A*S*H, I always came away proud because the series was powered by wonderful scripts and wonderful actors. I was constantly smiling inside whenever I was on the set. The episodes I directed included "The General's Practitioner," in which Alan Alda's character, Hawkeye, was considered for the job of personal doctor to a general; and "Lt. Radar O'Reilly," for which I was nominated for my second Emmy Award. The episode featured Radar (played by Gary Burghoff) whose promotion to lieutenant left him longing to be a corporal again.

At the Emmy Awards ceremony, I was nominated for best director of a situation comedy series, and Gary was nominated in the supporting actor category. That year they announced the winner in Gary's category before mine. When they announced that he had won, I felt a certain amount of encouragement for my own category. So, I was feeling rather confident when they started to read off the nominees for best director.

Next thing I knew they opened the envelop and said the name "Alan," at which point I stood up from my seat. However, the name "Alan" was then directly followed not by the name "Rafkin" but "Alda," who also was up for best director for another episode of M*A*S*H. At that point Alan Alda, who was sitting behind me, gently put his hand on my shoulder and sat me down before I made a complete ass of myself.

I was lying in bed the other night thinking about M*A*S*H. What really set the show apart for me was the incredibly positive attitude on the set. The cast and crew behaved like they were producing the best show on television. This attitude translated not into arrogance, but dedication. Everybody knew they were doing something special, and they wouldn't settle for anything less each week. On almost all the shows I've done the people involved worked very hard, but on M*A*S*H that effort was taken to a higher level. There was a quality about the show that was rare.

In 1975, five years after I had my heart attack on the set of *How to Frame a Fig*, I was on a tennis court when I experienced another weird sensation. I was trying to concentrate on my ground strokes but was

distracted by a series of symmetrical pains along my jaw line. I waited
to see if the pains would travel down my neck, but they stopped at my
jaw. I thought maybe it was a toothache, or something along those lines
that I could put off until I had time to visit the dentist. But the fact that
the pain was symmetrical began to nag at me. I decided to go to the
doctor.

"What do you think is wrong?" I asked my doctor.

"You need heart bypass surgery."

"When?"

"Now."

"Well, I'll call and make an appointment," I said, trying to figure
out when I might be able to squeeze the time into my busy directing
schedule.

"No. I mean *right* now. I'll call the ambulance," said the doctor as
he reached for the phone.

The ambulance took me to St. Joseph's Hospital in Burbank. I don't
remember being frightened during the ride, although I had every reason to be. Everything was happening too quickly for me to stop and an-
alyze it. But I will never forget the date of that heart surgery because it
also happened to be my daughter Leigh's birthday, which is February 3.

After the surgery I was placed in intensive care and later moved to
a private room. One day Saul Turteltaub and Bernie Ornstein, the producers of *Sanford and Son*, came to visit me. I remember being terribly
embarrassed by my condition and instinctively feeling that I should try
and deny it. I felt that admitting to heart surgery would be owning up
to a weakness that would make me less desirable as a director. I didn't
want to be passed over for jobs because of my weak ticker.

When Saul and Bernie walked into my room, I looked up, with
tubes hanging from every orifice of my body and said, "I had a hernia
operation. It's nothing serious." Obviously they knew I was lying.
My room was on a floor clearly marked for heart patients, but I just
couldn't admit it. Saul and Bernie just smiled knowingly at me.

I went back to work directing *Sanford and Son* five weeks after my
bypass surgery. I couldn't return to the set fast enough. I felt I had
wasted so much time sitting around in a hospital bed that now I would
have to make up for lost time.

6.

Sailing with the Love Boat and Some of Sitcom's Funniest Women

As long as I live, I will never forget what it feels like to be inside a studio soundstage. The soundstage for me has been a haven, a heaven, and a hell. When you first open the outside door of a stage, you are immediately confronted with a forbidding thick second door. The small space in between the two doors, enough for about three or four people to stand shoulder to shoulder, separates the fresh air of reality from the stale air of the make-believe sitcom world. If a small red light above the inside door is on, you must wait because a live recording is taking place. If the light is out, you can go ahead, never knowing for sure what you will find inside.

Some stages are bigger than others, but they're all basically huge cavernous buildings with four walls. If you're directing a three-camera sitcom, there will be bleachers for the audience and facing the bleachers will be several permanent sets. (On the other hand, if you're directing a movie or single-camera TV series, there is no audience and thus no need for the bleachers.) The sets vary from show to show. For example, on *Seinfeld* there might be the interior of Jerry's apartment, the coffee shop, and maybe several swing sets that are not there every week, but are written into the script for certain episodes.

Most of the soundstages I've worked on are old, dark, damp, and cold, particularly in the mornings before all the lights have been turned on. When I was directing a show, I'd leave my house in the morning and it could be seventy-five degrees outside. I might be carrying a heavy jacket with me and my neighbors would stare at me and think I was crazy. By the time I entered the soundstage I would already need to put on my jacket because it would be so damp. Somebody on a stage is always suffering from a cold or allergy because the inside is so dirty. The dust clings to the walls along with the stories of all the TV series and movies that have been shot inside over the years.

Somewhere on every soundstage there is a craft service or food table. Some shows have a table filled with junk food, others with healthier selections, but usually coffee and pastries are a staple. In general, the food is paid for by the production company, which positions the table as a meeting place for cast and crew. Periodically throughout the day you can return to the table and find something new depending on the hour and day of the week.

The only thing that usually doesn't change is the sugar content. There will always be sugar at the table. I know because I've become somewhat hypoglycemic over the years. Once while directing an episode of *Coach*, I asked one of the craft service people if he could cut down on the sugar. The *Coach* table was always filled with doughnuts, pastries, cereal, and more sugar than you could ever imagine. I asked if perhaps instead of so many doughnuts, maybe fruit could be substituted. The caterer looked at me and said, "Mr. Rafkin, the crew would kill me. They love the sugar." Eventually I did start to see some additional fruit, but the doughnut volume never diminished.

I now realize that the set was like a little happy kingdom to me. For most of my career the soundstage was the one place where I felt the safest, the happiest, the funniest, the loudest, and probably the angriest. But no matter how I felt, it was still my place. Even when I was directing a series or a particular script that I didn't like (or taking heat from a studio or network executive), I could still enjoy being on the set and rehearsing with the actors.

Some shows you decide to direct for love, others for money. If you can do both at the same time, that's great, but usually you have to make a choice. My decision to direct *The Love Boat* helped put my daughters through college, pure and simple. It wasn't the most sophisticated or well-respected show, but it paid nice money so I took it.

The Love Boat had a quality all its own. I realize that quality could be described as fluff, puff, and cotton candy, but it was still unique and helped set the show apart from the rest. The episodes may have looked easy to produce, but in reality they were tough shows to shoot.

My first day as a director on the series didn't get off to the best start. After a full day of shooting, producer Aaron Spelling walked onto the set with his wife, Candy, and a bunch of other people. None of them looked happy. Aaron said they had seen the dailies (or footage from the day before) and they didn't like what they had seen. There was a problem.

When a director hears news like that, his stomach falls to the ground. Hard.

"Aaron, what's wrong?" I asked.

I thought maybe my shots were off. Or they didn't like my staging. Or perhaps I had missed something in the script.

"It's her hair," he said.

"What?" I asked.

"Lauren Tewes's hair," he explained. "It's all wrong. Candy and I don't like it. We chose the wrong style. It was our fault."

Lauren Tewes played Julie McCoy, *The Love Boat*'s perky cruise director.

"You don't like her hair?"

"We have to reshoot everything with Lauren in it," he announced. "We're going to redo her hair."

I remember not only being impressed by their willingness to admit that they had made a mistake, but also the fact they were prepared to spend the additional money to reshoot all of her scenes. As it turned out, hair styling was the least of Lauren's problems. She also was struggling with a drug problem. Sometimes I can be rather naive when it comes to recognizing the signs of drug use, but with Lauren the signs were painted in big bold letters. You couldn't miss them. And when she was whacked out of her mind on drugs, which was the majority of the time, she could be a pain in the neck to direct.

One morning we were doing an indoor scene on a bar onboard the ship and Lauren wasn't making any sense at all. Words were coming out of her mouth, but they either weren't in the right order, or weren't the right words altogether. We ended up having to loop in some more articulate lines later to cover her mistakes. Lauren could be so rude when she was under the influence, but I understand that she eventually straightened herself out. I'm sure she's a nicer person for it.

▼ ▄▀ ▄▀ ▄▀ ▲

Primarily I directed episodes of *The Love Boat* that involved going out to sea. Other episodes were shot on a soundstage at Twentieth Century-Fox where they had built a forward deck and swimming pool. I preferred directing the episodes on the water because there was truly nothing like going out to sea. I shot the first cruise they ever did to Mexico and the ship stopped at every little town with a T-shirt for sale. It was relatively smooth sailing for the cast and crew until one day when we got into trouble. Big trouble.

Suzanne Somers was a guest star on the show that week and I wanted to shoot her and some of the other passengers coming back on the boat from a shopping trip in a Mexican port. So, we set up the shot on the pier. I was about to yell "Action!" when suddenly I saw two jeeps with four soldiers in each car racing toward us. No two soldiers were wearing the same uniform, but all of them seemed to be yelling and screaming at us in Spanish.

For a few minutes there was chaos on the set and nobody seemed to understand what crime we had committed. The soldiers took away our film and held it hostage until their demands were met. As it turned out, *The Love Boat*'s production company hadn't secured the proper permits to shoot on the pier. After a $40,000 "ransom" was paid, we got our film back and were able to complete the episode. It was an unforgettable shake down, but after that we never had much trouble in Mexico.

I directed a number of *Love Boat* cruises to Mexico, and frankly I don't care much if I ever see Mexico again. But as a director I was never treated better than I was by Spelling and his company. In particular, I got along very well with Doug Cramer, the series' executive producer, who went on many of the cruises with us. Sometimes I also brought along my daughters. Even though I was working most of the time, it was still nice to have the girls traveling with me.

Aside from Lauren Tewes, the permanent cast of *The Love Boat* was a pleasure to direct. Fred Grandy, who played the amiable purser named Gopher, was a bright and very funny young man. He later left acting for a career in politics (as a congressman from Iowa), which didn't surprise me because on the set we often talked about politics. He also had a magnificent sense of humor and an uncanny ear for dialects. I enjoyed just clowning around with him in between takes.

Fred and the rest of the cast were very professional people. They showed up on time, learned their lines, and took their jobs seriously, but not themselves. One of the joys of *The Love Boat* was Gavin MacLeod, who played Captain Merrill Stubing. I use the word joy because Gavin was so thrilled and delighted to be in the series; he was not only captain of the ship, but truly the leader of the cast. There was a peace and tranquility about him that kept what could have been a very hectic schedule from getting out of control.

The odd thing about directing *The Love Boat* was in working with a new batch of actors every week. None of the guest stars was ever really in the groove of having done the series before, but most were grateful just to be working. I guess in the old days you would have called them "B" movie stars. I won't mention names. You've all seen episodes of *The Love Boat.* The cruises were filled with people who were once famous, could have been famous, or who were on their way to not being famous anymore. For them, *The Love Boat* offered a way to keep their careers afloat.

In my opinion the series was based on a wonderful concept and was wonderfully done. We worked very hard on *The Love Boat* and I think that comes across when you look back and see the places we traveled to and the extreme way we shot the scenes. We strove to capture the bluest blue and the greenest green whenever we made a port call. Although directing *The Love Boat* was not the kind of career move that brought me closer to winning an Emmy award, I loved doing the series and have very fond memories of the experience.

The relatively calm waters I experienced while directing *The Love Boat* unfortunately did nothing to prepare me for the rough ride I would have on *Laverne & Shirley* with stars Penny Marshall and Cindy Williams. It was one of the most unpleasant series I have ever directed. The experience was softened by the fact that *Laverne & Shirley* made me a lot of money in residuals and certainly taught me a great deal about directing women.

Since the series went off the air in 1983 after eight seasons, both Penny and Cindy have grown considerably, much to my pleasant surprise. They've almost undergone a metamorphosis. Penny is now a mature, gracious and well-respected film director (*Big* and *A League of Their Own*), and Cindy is a wife, mother, actress, and film producer (*Father of the Bride*). But during *Laverne & Shirley*, the two were terrors to work with.

I first directed Penny in 1974 in a forgettable series called *Paul Sand in Friends and Lovers.*

I worked with her again when I was hired to direct *Laverne & Shirley*, a spin-off of Garry Marshall's successful series *Happy Days*. Laverne and Shirley first made their debut on *Happy Days* during a double date with Richie and Fonzie (Ron Howard and Henry Winkler). I came on board to direct *Laverne & Shirley* in its second and third years, when it was already a ratings hit.

One of the biggest problems I faced as a director was that neither Penny nor Cindy wanted to rehearse. And they weren't all that thrilled with coming out of their dressing rooms. There was only one person, the first assistant director, Linda McMurray, who had a good track record of persuading the two stars to come onto the set. I don't know who was taking what, but the buzz on the set was that there were drugs available for those who wanted them.

Although some people on *Laverne & Shirley* had reason to party, I was certainly not having a very good time on the show. Directing the series was like pulling teeth. Penny and Cindy were undisciplined and bratty as were some members of the supporting cast. At one point we were sitting down at a table (during a rare rehearsal) when David Lander (who played Squiggy) threw the script down and said, "This is shit!" Penny and Cindy said they agreed. I knew I was losing control of the show, which is the worst thing that can happen to a director. So, to regain some ground, I called producer Garry Marshall (who also happened to be Penny's older brother) and asked him to come over to the set to intervene.

Garry had always been a very even-tempered man to work with; this was the one and only time I ever saw him lose it. He told all of the actors that, in essence, if they weren't happy with the material, they could just walk out the stage door. He would pay them for every episode left on their contract, but things just couldn't continue this way. Right then and there, Garry said, the actors had to stop denigrating the material. After Garry left the stage, the actors behaved themselves for about . . . an hour and eight minutes. Then we were right back where we started.

Despite the problems, we did have some fun on the set of *Laverne & Shirley*. I was particularly amused by the characters of Lenny and Squiggy, played by Michael McKean and the previously mentioned Lander. The men had developed similar characters while students at Carnegie Mellon University, and they could make me laugh endlessly. The script would call for Penny or Cindy to say a line like, "What imbeciles would do a thing like that?" Then suddenly the front door to their apartment would swing open and Lenny and Squiggy would enter with their trademark, "HEEELLLOOO!"

What always amazed me was that as little as all the show's actors rehearsed the material, they usually were right on target by Tuesday night when we went before the cameras and studio audience. Then they worked their buns off and, like magic, everything clicked. Garry Marshall would do the warm-up, and the energy was always high because the audience was made up of people who really wanted to see the show. They were fans from all over the country who had waited weeks, sometimes even months, to get tickets. They just loved *Laverne & Shirley*.

In addition to the energy of show night, another aspect of the series that I enjoyed was that each week the script presented a new adventure for the two women. One week they'd be on roller skates. Another week it would be ice skates. If they weren't wrestling, then they'd be boxing or doing some other sport. And this kind of physical humor isn't a breeze to shoot either. It takes time. Sometimes on show nights we'd be there until two in the morning doing pick-ups of shots that I wasn't able to get while the studio audience was there. Penny and Cindy would be exhausted, but if I said, "Let's do it again," they would be ready. For that kind of stamina, I admired them a lot.

I'd be a liar if I said I ran the show when I directed it. I certainly staged Penny and Cindy and gave them what direction I could, but those two women ran the show and they called the shots (sometimes even bringing people to tears, like the wardrobe woman). They intimidated and frustrated me to the point that I kept plastic garbage cans back-stage so I could kick them. I suppose one explanation for the tension on the set could have been that fame had come in with such a rush for Penny and Cindy. One minute they were struggling actresses and the next they were on the number one show in America.

After the first few seasons they turned their antagonistic attitudes on each other. They became extremely competitive and if one got some-thing, the other wanted it right away, too, or there would be hell to pay. They had begun the show as friends, but they evolved into what looked like enemies. I heard about later episodes in which they would stand around counting and tallying up punch lines just to make sure no one was getting an unfair advantage. After a while, it wasn't enough that they didn't like each other, Penny and Cindy seemed to decide in ironic unison that they didn't like what they were doing either.

After eight seasons, *Laverne & Shirley* went off the air and Penny and Cindy went onto bigger, and ultimately much better, things. I would later have pleasant meetings with both women. I was a director on the TV series *Hope and Gloria*, when I ran into Cindy Williams backstage. She was appearing as a guest star, but unfortunately I was off the show that week so I didn't get to direct her. She ran over to me and gave me a big hug. We talked for a little while and she told me how happy she was with her husband, Bill Hudson, and their children. It was clear she had grown as an actor and a person.

I ran into Penny years later at the Pritikin Center, a place known for helping people lose weight, stop smoking, and overcome a variety of other addictions. I was visiting an old comic friend of mine who was there trying to lose weight. As I was having dinner with my friend, Penny came over to the table. She was also a guest at the center and was trying to kick her long-time smoking habit. That evening, she could not have been more gracious.

I ran into Penny again along Carbon Beach in Malibu, where I had lived for more than twenty years. Her brother Garry has a home on the beach and Penny was walking along the sand when she saw me. The sun was behind her and I didn't realize who it was until she sat down beside me and said, "Hello." She had a smile on her face and we talked for a while. Penny has not only turned into a fine director, but a really nice person. I'm happy for that.

Sometimes now I'll be doing my stretching exercises in front of the television and I'll catch an old rerun of *Laverne & Shirley*. I'll be lying on the floor, laughing to myself and saying, "Yep. That was funny." I laugh and laugh all the way to the bank. The money I continue to receive from *Laverne & Shirley* helped build my house in Montana and pay for my twenty-two-foot power boat *Residuals*. Not bad for putting up with two of sitcom's funniest, but most difficult, ladies.

Another woman I directed around this time was Linda Lavin in the TV series *Alice*. The show was based on the movie *Alice Doesn't Live Here Anymore*, about an aspiring singer who works as a waitress in a diner to support her young son. I directed *Alice* off and on for two years. During that time I quickly discovered that although Linda was a very talented actress, she could be difficult to work with just like Penny and Cindy.

It wasn't surprising that some of television's funniest women were also some of the most difficult people, because they were usually caught in a power struggle. On one side was a talented, strong-willed actress and on the other side was a group of very opinionated, mostly male, producers who held the purse strings. The rest of the cast and crew were stuck between the two, waiting to see whom to pledge their allegiance to. Some people drifted closer to the star, others to the producers. That's the way it was in the late 1970s and that's the way it continues to be today on series like *Roseanne, Murphy Brown,* and *Cybill.* I saw Linda in *Broadway Bound,* a Neil Simon play. After the audience had left, I was still sitting, stunned by her thrilling performance. Talking to Linda, I realized how she has matured and mellowed since *Alice.* Now she's a great talent with a full life.

One week on *Alice* we had a rather strange incident before a Friday night show. I was standing backstage experiencing my usual preshow flop sweat attack when I noticed a strange man standing near Linda's dressing room. I sensed that something wasn't quite right about the man so I walked over to him.

"May I help you?" I asked.

"Yeah," he said. "Linda wanted to see me. Do you know where I can find her?"

"Of course," I said, trying to keep my voice calm. "I'll tell her you're here."

"No. No," he said. "I'll find her myself."

"Please, I'll go and get her for you," I said. "Just wait right here."

I ducked into a nearby dressing room and phoned security. They arrived in time to grab the man, who turned out to be a weirdo with a big knife. I have no idea what his intent was, but the experience was very frightening. It amazes me that with all of the security on studio lots, determined strangers still manage to get in. I suppose it's because soundstages are so large that it's nearly impossible to completely secure all of the entrances every minute of the day.

Today many actresses have taken security into their own hands by hiring full-time bodyguards, and I can't really blame them. Candice Bergen, whom I later directed on *Murphy Brown,* has a bodyguard and also has helped develop a unique security system on her set. When you come onto the stage of *Murphy Brown,* you must walk through a metal detector and past at least two security guards who sometimes even frisk people. One of the guards gives each legitimate employee or visitor a round dot. Each day a different color dot is handed out, and you're supposed to wear the dot on your clothing so it's visible. You are then free to come and go as you wish and security will know that you are part of the crew.

It's unfortunate that security on studio lots has to be so tight, but the reality is that some fans become so unreasonably obsessed with television actors and actresses that they threaten and sometimes follow through on acts of violence. I saw it happen while I was directing the series *One Day at a Time*. On show nights sometimes I would do the warm-up in front of the studio audience. It was fun, and it reminded me of when I used to do stand-up comedy in the army. One night the warm-up nearly turned into a disaster.

I had been doing the warm-up for so long at this point, that I knew almost every word backwards and forwards. I was so secure with the act that I started to let my eyes wander up into the bleachers. I was browsing through the faces in the audience when I noticed a man sitting near the front row wearing army fatigues. Suddenly something clicked in my mind: I had been told earlier by security that Valerie Bertinelli, who played Barbara on the series, had received several threatening fan letters. The author of the letters said he was going to kill Valerie in the name of Jesus Christ.

In the middle of one of my jokes, I suddenly got the feeling that the man in the fatigues was the person who had written the letters to Valerie. I immediately stopped my act, put down the microphone, and abruptly walked off stage. I quickly called security, who followed my suggestion and quietly plucked the man out of the audience. It turned out that my instincts were right and he was indeed the man who had been threatening Valerie. Luckily, in this case the tragedy was stopped in time. Unfortunately, other television stars have not been so fortunate and have been physically hurt and even killed.

One of the neatest members of television's batch of funny ladies I directed in a sitcom was Valerie Harper on the series *Rhoda*. I had directed her in several episodes of *The Mary Tyler Moore Show*, and when her character Rhoda Morgenstern was spun-off into her own series I was hired to do some of those episodes as well.

I remember that I hadn't been there too long when Valerie brought in Viola Spolin, a teacher and legend in theater circles, particularly Chicago. Viola led the cast in what we called "theater games," which we would do before rehearsal every day. Basically they were weird exercises to loosen us up and try to break down any of the actors' inhibitions. When Viola first arrived and started wiggling and giggling around the set I was the first one to scoff at her. What does this have to do with acting, I thought to myself. But after the first session the cast seemed somehow more connected for the rest of the day. The bond that existed between us was strengthened as a result of the games.

In addition to Valerie, another wonderful member of the cast was Julie Kavner, who has since gone on to star in several Woody Allen films. (She also was in Tracey Ullman's TV series, which I think was one of the best shows ever on the air.) At the time we shot *Rhoda*, Julie was just finding herself as an actress and was quite happy to play second banana to Valerie as Rhoda's whiny sister Brenda. Julie was always a pleasure to work with on the set and a wonderful human being as well.

I think overall that the cast and crew had a pretty good time working on *Rhoda*. Many of the producers socialized with Valerie and other members of the cast off the set. There really wasn't a problematic person among us, except perhaps actor David Groh, who played Valerie's screen husband, Joe. David was a pain in the ass and to make things worse, he had no sense of humor. He was under this bizarre misconception that *Rhoda* was a drama instead of a comedy. In my opinion, he brought the show down around him by trying to turn every joke into some hard piece of drama. He just wasn't on the same wavelength as the rest of us.

During the late 1970s while I directed many female comedians, I also directed several sitcoms about minorities including *What's Happening*, an African-American series starring Ernest Thomas, Fred Berry, and Haywood Nelson. Haywood was a really good kid and Ernest was an excellent actor. But on *What's Happening*, Fred Berry was the one to look out for. He could be trouble.

Fred was an overweight boy who played a character named Rerun, the clown of the series. He received many of the show's big laughs. Unfortunately, he later had some personal problems that carried over onto the set. After I had left the show, there was a big contract dispute and I was told that Fred was the instigator behind the trouble that followed. He convinced Ernest and Haywood to join him in a strike for more money. Eventually, the producers simply had enough of the boys' antics and they closed the series down.

Another minority series I directed was called *Viva Valdez*. The series had the distinction of being one of the first Latino sitcoms ever on the air and was produced by Bernie Rothman and Jack Wohl. To this day, Jack is a member of my poker game, which has been going on for at least twenty-five years. We play every Thursday when I'm in town.

What's interesting to me about this game is that it's one of the few bastions left where male bonding is permitted. We never socialize, but concentrate on the game and our camaraderie. We also try to be supportive of each other in good times and bad, like the time player Sid Tessler lost his eye to cancer. Following his cancer surgery, Sid wore a black patch over his eye for a short time. One Thursday night he arrived at the poker game to find the seven of us all wearing black eye patches as a show of support. Sid's healthy now and even runs in the Boston Marathon. And, of course, he still plays poker.

Back when Jack Wohl and Bernie Rothman were putting together *Viva Valdez*, the ABC representative was Marcy Carsey, who now along with Tom Werner produces shows such as *Roseanne, Home Improvement,* and *Third Rock from the Sun*. Although producing has now made her very happy (and very rich), Marcy was one of the best network reps that I've ever worked with. She was at the network during a time when it was difficult for women to make suggestions because many men treated them like they didn't know anything. But Marcy was bright, funny, and a good friend to all of us.

Viva Valdez didn't have quite as long a career as Marcy. The series was about a close-knit Mexican-American family living in East Los Angeles. The matriarch of the family was actress Carmen Zapata, who was probably the most famous Latina actress in Los Angeles working at the time. In reality, Carmen was from Argentina and many of the cast members were from countries other than Mexico. It was a running joke on the set that they were all playing members of a Mexican-American family, but no one was actually from Mexico.

Much to the disappointment of the cast and crew, the series never made it beyond one season. I think it probably could have used better writing, and a little more time to catch on and build a loyal following. I thought the cast was quite enchanting. And if *Viva Valdez* had worked, the series might have been able to make a positive mark on the Mexican-American community in Los Angeles. As it is now, the city is unfortunately so racially divided that a sitcom wouldn't be able to do much to repair the damage.

One of the best things *Viva Valdez* had going for it was its realistic sense of what it's like to live with a large extended family. If there was one thing missing from my life during the late 1970s, it was having a large family to share my career with. I had my two daughters, but I wanted to spend time every day with a family of mothers, brothers, aunts, and uncles. But I seemed to be jumping from sitcom to sitcom, never staying around long enough to make any long-term friendships.

I decided that maybe it was time that I set down some roots, commit to a series, and establish myself as a one-sitcom director (at least for a while). I had proven that I could come in, direct a few episodes, and then leave. But what would happen if I stuck around for a while? I soon found my answer and my new family on the series *One Day at a Time,* a show that appropriately had no regular father in the cast.

7.

Committing to More Than One Day at a Time

I was nominated for my third Emmy award in 1982 for an episode that I directed of *One Day at a Time*. After losing the nomination two previous times for *The Mary Tyler Moore Show* and *M*A*S*H*, I really didn't hold out much hope for winning on that night in September. The episode I was up for was called "Barbara's Crisis" featuring actress Valerie Bertinelli and her character's battle with endometriosis. Although there was no doubt I was proud of the episode, after looking at the competition, I thought I had the least chance of winning. But wouldn't you know it, I won. I finally won.

I have seen a video tape that my kids made of me accepting the award. To some people I probably look like just another director going up to accept an award. But I think I look like a gorilla. An angry gorilla. Many times I have looked at myself walking up to the podium and am fascinated by the fact that I am muttering something under my breath. I had this dazed look on my face as I was mumbling, "Yeah. God damn it. You're God damn right. I won. God damn it. Yeah!" But I wasn't just babbling to myself. I was talking to my father. Even though he had passed away many years before, I was talking to my father.

When I finally arrived at the podium I looked out at the crowd and asked, "Is there a paramedic around?" Some of my friends at home who were watching the ceremony thought I was having a heart attack. It was only a joke, but obviously not a very good one if it scared people instead of making them laugh. But the award would prove to be one of the high points of my life. It made me feel that I was a success at some-

The advertisement that appeared in the trade papers when I won my Emmy for an episode of *One Day at a Time*, 1982. *Courtesy of Columbia TriStar Television.*

thing. The only regret that I had was that my father was not there to see me accept the award. In his eyes, I don't think I was ever a success at anything. And when I finally did something that he wouldn't have been able to deny, he was already dead.

My father never had any confidence in me as a director. I remember at the beginning of my career when I called my father and told him that CBS had made me a director and was sending me to live in California his comment was, "What the hell do you think you know about directing?"

"But Dad, they are going to pay me $752 a week. Isn't that great?" I asked.

"They'll find out about you in three weeks!" he said, discounting the whole thing.

A shrink might say my father was probably jealous because show business seemed like such an exotic and fascinating world compared to his own clothing business. But his attitude made me feel like a phony and a fake most of the time. For years after I moved to Los Angeles, no matter how much money I was making or how much fun I was having, I was always afraid that I would be found out. I worried that one day, when I least expected it, a network president was going to look down at his list of directors and say, "Alan Rafkin? We're paying him how much? He's got no talent. Get rid of him. We can get somebody else a lot better for a lot cheaper." And then they'd add, "And his father was right!"

It wasn't until the early 1980s that I began to understand, with the help of therapy, that I was good at what I did for a living. But sometimes, no matter how many actors praised me or how many executives said they appreciated my work, I heard my father's voice shooting an arrow full of doubt in my direction. The night that I won the Emmy for *One Day at a Time* was the first moment in my career that the anxiety and pain lifted, allowing me room to breathe. It was nice, even if it was only temporary.

One Day at a Time was one of the first single-parent sitcoms on television. The show ran from 1974 until 1985 and starred Bonnie Franklin as the mother, Ann Romano. The other regular cast members were Valerie Bertinelli as her youngest daughter Barbara Cooper and Pat

Harrington, Jr., as Dwayne Schneider, the building's superintendent. Mackenzie Phillips played Ann's older daughter Julie Cooper on and off throughout the run of the series.

I came on to direct the series when it was beginning its third year, and I stayed through its eighth year. Back then it was the longest block of time I had ever been associated with a sitcom and for that reason it stands out as a milestone in my career. The series was also important to me because it represented my first experience with legendary comedy producer Norman Lear.

Norman was an exciting producer to work for. When you said that you worked on a Norman Lear sitcom it was like saying that you had hit the big league as far as comedy television went. He created *All in the Family*, which debuted in 1971. If Norman had never created another TV series in his life, he would have been remembered as the man who sent television in a new direction by giving depth and bite to the phrase "family sitcom."

The impressive thing was that Norman didn't stop at *All in the Family*. He went on to produce a stable of other sitcoms such as *Maude, Good Times, The Jeffersons, Sanford and Son,* and the quirky *Mary Hartman, Mary Hartman.* At the time I joined *One Day at a Time*, Norman had something like six TV series on the air. Despite his success, he had to woo me to come and direct *One Day at a Time* because I was also being courted by the producers of *Three's Company*. It was hectic, yet exhilarating, to have a breakfast meeting with the people from *Three's Company*, and then meet with Norman in the afternoon to discuss his show.

I was trying to weigh the pros and cons of both offers when one afternoon Norman decided it for me. "Okay," he said, "we'll not only make you director, but we'll also make you an executive producer of *One Day at a Time*." I hadn't been an executive producer since working on *Love, American Style* in the early 1970s. The length of time was just enough to make me forget what a headache the job had been and make me fond of the title again. So, I said to Norman, "I'm your man."

▬ ▬ ▬ ▬ ▲

The thing about a TV series that runs for nearly ten years is that the cast and crew become like a family because you spend more time with them than your own family. Because I was looking for a larger family to spend time with, that was fine with me. I wanted to not only work hard and put in long hours, but to spend those hours with people I could connect with. People I could be friends with. People who would see me as a director, a father, and a friend. I think that's why it was so difficult when one of my "children" struggled so desperately with a drug problem.

Mackenzie Phillips was one of the brightest young actresses I have ever worked with. Yet she was also one of the most unfortunate ones. Her life turned out to be worse than any soap opera. She not only had a rough family life growing up, she had less support in her life than any other human being I have ever come upon. So, it was not surprising that a person with so little support would become vulnerable and an easy target for addiction.

From what I heard on the set, Mackenzie's father, John Phillips (a singer in the 1960s musical group the Mamas & the Papas), turned her onto drugs when she was young, some said as young as nine years old. Rumor had it that he congratulated her when she was arrested for the first time for possession. With a father like that, it was not surprising that the daughter developed a drug habit. That family seemed to use drugs like other families consume breakfast cereal.

When Mackenzie was using drugs, which probably was most of the time when I first joined the TV series, she was extremely difficult to get along with. She was never nasty like some people who use drugs can be, but her thoughts seemed on a different plane from the rest of ours. It was frustrating to give her direction on a scene because I never knew if she was processing the information or merely letting it float over her head like a cloud passing by.

One time we were rehearsing a scene and I looked up to see Mackenzie hopping from one leg to another. She wasn't able to stand still. I was finally so distracted that I had to say something.

"Mac," I said, "you've got to stand still for a minute!"

"I am standing still," she said as she hopped over to her other leg.

I think we all tried to ignore her problem, wishing that one day it would just go away. But it began to interfere with her work more and more. One day the producers told me that the next time Mac came to work "under the influence," I was to put her in a limousine that would be on call, and send her to a doctor they had contacted. I hated the idea of being a policeman for anybody. But it looked like something had to be done, and as the director I was the obvious choice to make the call.

Mackenzie came in one Friday, which was show night, and I knew by looking at her that this was going to be the day I would have to send her to the doctor. She literally was holding onto the wall just to keep herself upright. She said she had been awake all night, but promised that as soon as she had some breakfast she would be as good as new. Anybody who watched *One Day at a Time* regularly during the first few years of the series will remember how thin Mackenzie was. Aside from genetics, part of the reason for her being underweight was her unusual diet. Breakfast was traditionally apple juice or V-8 juice with a pickle. The meal was usually brought to her by her then husband.

Her husband, who has since and not surprisingly become her ex-husband, was a creep as well as a drug pusher in my book. Mackenzie said later, after she had cleaned herself up from the drugs, that her primary reason for marrying the guy was because the relationship provided her with "a fast and easy way to get drugs." That Friday I remember her husband came in to bring her the "breakfast" and they both disappeared into her dressing room. I don't know what exactly they did in there, but about a half hour later, she came out peppy as can be.

I picked up the phone, called the limousine, and alerted the doctor. As I ushered her into the limo she started to scream at me and call me names. I hated doing it, but I was just trying to do my job because she so clearly wasn't up to doing her own.

Following the incident, Mackenzie was off the series for a year or two. After that, she returned briefly only to leave a little while later for good. Her personal problems were apparently too deep and complex to work out on the soundstage of a sitcom. It was a shame because I always thought she was very talented.

I've seen Mackenzie on and off in recent years. When we worked together on the series, she looked as fragile as a piece of paper. Today she looks like a million bucks. She has two children and the last time I saw her she was in a very happy and healthy relationship. Now that she seems to have her life in order, nothing would make me happier than if I could make her seventeen years old again and give her another shot at *One Day at a Time*. She was somebody who always deserved one clean chance at life. I think she's finally given herself that chance.

⬛⬛⬛⬛

Valerie Bertinelli was cast in *One Day at a Time* when she was no more than thirteen years old. By the time I arrived she had celebrated her fifteenth birthday and was a beautiful, funny, and delightful young woman. No matter how pretty she looked on the outside, though, I always had the suspicion that trapped inside Valerie was a fat Italian lady who was going to have nine children and be the beloved matriarch of a big family.

As it turned out, she married rock musician Eddie Van Halen. Before they were married, Eddie would come around the set of *One Day at a Time* on Friday nights when we were shooting in front of the audience. Whenever he was there, the bleachers would be filled with not only fans of our series but also many of Eddie's groupies. Every once in a while he would come out from back stage and wave or take a bow in front of the audience. His fans would go nuts. But most of the time he tried to keep a low profile.

Different from the way you would picture a rock star to be, Eddie was a very nice young man. One time Valerie invited my daughters and me to a Van Halen concert and she cautioned, "Alan, I would suggest that you wear ear plugs." I thought she was kidding, but after sitting through a Van Halen concert I think ear plugs would have been a wise investment.

The concert was at the Los Angeles Forum, and it was a real treat to be able to bring my teenage daughters along. We had fantastic seats (which easily won me some points with my girls) and they had a great time. From my perspective, though, I thought the concert was a little dangerous. Having had major heart surgery, it was frightening feeling the beat of the music as it ricocheted from my head to my toes. But watching Eddie live on stage bouncing around was also rather exciting (even for a dad).

There was an empty seat next to one of the girls, and about half way through the concert a man drifted into our row and took the seat. I thought he was harmless until I noticed that he was smoking a joint. It wouldn't have been so bad if he hadn't leaned over and offered the joint to my daughters. I tried to stay calm as I poked my head around the girls and gave the guy my best stern "father" look telling him to cut it out. The three of us haven't attended another rock concert together, but our trip to see Van Halen was certainly memorable.

Over the years Valerie has continued to work in TV on several miniseries, movies-of-the-week, and a few sitcoms including the short-lived *Café American* (where my daughter Dru coincidentally worked as a script supervisor). Valerie never did have the nine children that I thought she would, but she is still married to Eddie and they now have a son named Wolfgang. Career aspirations aside, I think I was right about one thing about Valerie. Family was always extremely important to her, and I'm so happy that she finally has one of her own.

Shortly after I made the decision to direct *One Day at a Time*, I went to see a stage production of *The Owl and the Pussy Cat* starring Bonnie Franklin and directed by her manager, Marilyn Shapiro. Because I was going to be working with Bonnie on the series in a few weeks, I wanted to see what she was like during a performance. As I sat in the audience watching Bonnie up on stage I thought to myself, "What the hell have I gotten myself into?"

Bonnie was from what I call the "slapping" school of acting. Whenever she wanted to get a point across she would slap her forehead with her palm, slap her thigh with her hand, or slap both hands on her hips. To me, Bonnie took overreacting to a new level. I had already signed my deal with Norman Lear to direct *One Day at a Time*, and now I knew I would have my work cut out for me.

The first day I went into rehearsal for the series, I was surprised to find Marilyn Shapiro (the woman responsible for directing the play I had loathed so much) sitting in the rehearsal hall. Most directors don't allow (or at least don't appreciate) agents and managers sitting in on rehearsals. It's different if they come to watch a run-through once in a while because then the director has already had time to work privately with the actor on most of the rough spots. But rehearsals can sometimes be very raw, and agents and managers do little but stir up the pot. To make things worse, Marilyn was one of those people who, even when she was content, didn't wear a pleasant look on her face.

I opted to take my problem with Marilyn right to the top, to producer Norman Lear. I described Marilyn as a woman who threw a pall over everything. She could look like she was smelling something bad even if there was no odor in the room. In addition, after each scene Bonnie would rush over to Marilyn to discuss it. I found their little side conferences unproductive and sometimes destructive.

Norman told me that unfortunately there was little he could do. It was already the third year of the series and I was looked upon as the newcomer. The stage had already been set and the actors cast. Marilyn had been there for all three years and didn't show any signs of moving on. So I had to live with the arrangement, even though it made me and other members of the cast (whose agents and managers weren't able to stand guard) very uncomfortable.

Sometimes you become better friends with the supporting cast rather than the stars and that was the case with me and Pat Harrington, Jr., who played Schneider. Like Nancy Walker, Pat Harrington, Jr.'s father was a vaudeville star. In addition, Pat Harrington, Sr., owned a Manhattan night club. Ironically, years earlier when I was still the assistant director on *The Verdict Is Yours* in New York, Pat's father appeared in an episode. Little did I know that years later I would be living in Hollywood, directing his son in a sitcom, and becoming the best of friends with him.

Pat Harrington, Sr., would have been proud of the fact that as an actor his son had a brilliant ear for whatever character he was doing. Most people probably first saw Pat when he appeared on the old Jack Paar *Tonight Show* as Guido Panzini, the Italian golf pro. Pat did such a good job with the accent that many viewers thought he really was Italian. I thought he was hysterically funny.

Unfortunately I don't think that the writers on *One Day at a Time* were able to do Pat's talent justice. They didn't really know how to integrate Schneider's character into the Cooper family. So they either wrote an entire episode that centered around Schneider (which was not very often), or hardly wrote him in at all. Pat once told me that he hated having to open the Coopers' apartment door, walk in, do four or five jokes in a row like a monologue, and then leave. And I don't blame him. That's not the kind of work any actor finds challenging.

Pat ended up writing and rewriting a lot of his own material, but the scripts were still very limiting to him, which was a shame. But thanks to the series, Pat and I became friends and remain friends today. In fact, we belong to a group called Yarmy's Army, which is one of the most compassionate things to ever come out of our industry.

This army, or band of comedians and other men who make their living through comedy, was named for character actor Dick Yarmy, who was Don Adams's brother. I used Dick in many of the sitcoms I directed, particularly *M*A*S*H*. He was a wonderful human being and one of those rare actors who was comfortable with his career even though he knew that he was never going to become a big star. He did his work and made a living and only had one weakness: horses. Dick loved to go to the race track. There were several times when he missed auditions and his agent couldn't find him. He was usually at the track.

Unfortunately, Dick's life was turned upside down when he was diagnosed with throat cancer. After he found out about his disease, a few of his friends started taking him out to dinner on Tuesday nights to cheer him up. He'd sit at the head of the table and they'd tell stories, try out jokes, and do whatever they could to keep Dick's mind off his troubles. After a while, word started getting around that the dinners not only helped lift Dick's spirits, but his companions' as well. The group enlarged to about ten people and then it started to really take off. I soon became a regular member, along with Pat Harrington, Jr. Near the end, when Dick was so sick that he could hardly speak, he could still laugh, and that meant everything to him.

And then one Tuesday, Dick was no longer at the head of the table. The cancer he battled finally killed him. Instead of a memorial service, his friends celebrated his life with a hilarious and uplifting ceremony. It glorified the memory of Dick and what he was all about. I remember after the service, I had a strange feeling that I was not only going to miss Dick, but also getting together with his group of friends. I started talking to some of the others, and it turned out that many of them felt the same way. We didn't want to say goodbye.

That's when we decided to keep the group together. Today there are still about thirty of us, and we meet for dinner the second Tuesday of each month. The evening starts off with a toast to Dick, and then we get down to the business of making each other laugh. The group is very eclectic and includes television comedians such as Don Knotts and Shelley Berman as well as voice-over actors Tom Sharp and Ronnie Schell, who work in commercials. Sometimes there's an invited guest (such as a prominent producer or a comedian who hasn't worked in a while) and other times it's just us. But we always end up having a thoroughly good time, and we all feel somewhere up there Dick is laughing too.

On *One Day at a Time* the work habits of the cast were very good because Bonnie Franklin was a professional when it came to work. No one tried harder, worked longer, or came in more prepared than Bonnie. We usually got a new script on Friday night or Saturday morning. On Monday when we arrived and first sat down to go over the script, you could always look over to see Bonnie's script filled with handwritten notes. During our meetings, she would share some thoughts about her character, or make suggestions about someone else's character. She always gave her notes in a very gracious manner. Everyone knew that as the star of the series she was the boss. But it was the accuracy of her notes and the gentle way that they were given that made people listen to her.

On *One Day at a Time* we rehearsed often and worked very hard, but we also laughed a lot. We even put together a band and played during our lunch hour for a couple of years. Even though Pat Harrington, Jr., was a wonderful piano player, as a joke he played this really bad piano, like the kind you hear in funky cocktail lounges. Actor Michael

Lembeck (who played MacKenzie's husband on the series and is now a TV director himself) was our bass player and Boyd Gaines (who played Valerie's husband) played guitar. I came in on the drums. We all gathered at lunch to play some really bad music, but it was enjoyable and very funny.

Sometimes when you work on a sitcom you can have the pleasure of watching other actors and actresses on the soundstages or rehearsal halls around you. We were rehearsing in a hall at Universal Studios (where we shot the show for part of its run) when we heard there was a musical special rehearsing next door. The curiosity was killing us so we peeked to see who was in the special.

We were thrilled to find that it was none other than one of Hollywood's sexiest women and one of ballet's greatest stars: Ann-Margret and Mikhail Baryshnikov. There was a small common door in the back of our rehearsal hall that separated our space from theirs. Whenever we knew they were rehearsing, we would hover around the door, trying to sneak furtive peeks at the action inside. If one of the stars looked up, or another member of the crew looked toward the door, we would quickly retreat and shut the door.

One morning I was coming up in the elevator when I looked over to find myself standing next to Baryshnikov. There was nobody else in the elevator, so I introduced myself to him.

"Hello, I'm Alan Rafkin," I offered.

"Oh, you are the director of *One Day at a Time*," he said in his thick Russian accent.

"Yes, I am."

"If you promise to stop opening and closing the door so much today, at the end of the day when we are finished rehearsing we will do a whole musical number for you," he said.

"That would be terrific," I said, embarrassed and thrilled at the same time.

I went back and told my cast and crew that if we could try and be good boys and girls, we would be rewarded. At the end of the day, after remaining on our best behavior, we all shuffled through the connecting door to watch our special performance. Ann-Margret was nothing but absolutely gorgeous and gracious. And as for Baryshnikov, meeting him made it clear to me why women flip for him. He is one of the most charming men I've ever met in my life. The musical number they did for us that day was, as expected, sensational. After we finished applauding profusely, we turned around and all obediently headed back through the connecting door.

Another celebrity that the cast of *One Day at a Time* got to meet was *All in the Family*'s Jean Stapleton. Her son, John Putch, appeared as Valerie Bertinelli's spurned high school boyfriend in several episodes of our series. John was a very nice young man and wonderful to work with. Jean would sometimes visit the set and sit with me in the booth, where I oversaw the cameras as the show was shot on tape. When Jean was in the booth watching John below, she would giggle and laugh, so amused by his performance. It was heartwarming to see that the lady I knew to be such a fine actress was also such a proud mother.

Norman Lear was also a very proud and attentive parent to all of the shows that he produced. Somehow, no matter how many TV series he had on the air, he managed to get to every show for at least one rehearsal a week. He might drop by for a dress rehearsal or pop over for show night. No matter when it was, it demonstrated that he really cared about the shows he had created. He wanted to be supportive and his presence was always appreciated.

What I loved about Norman was not only his obvious talent as an administrator, but particularly his strength as a writer. He was part of a handful of producer-writers at the time who could sit down and rewrite or fix a scene on the spot if it wasn't working. And if I still didn't like what he came up with, I felt free to say, "Norman, that doesn't work either." And he'd come right back and say, "We'll make it better. We'll find a way."

When it came to the end of my tenure on *One Day at a Time*, Norman was nearing the end of his as well. He started to be around less and less and eventually sold his company and transferred the operations to a bunch of guys with Harvard MBAs. There are a lot of very good uses for a Harvard MBA, but producing and writing jokes for a sitcom is not one of them. Two of the men who took over for Norman on *One Day at a Time* were named Alan Horn and Glen Padnick. Today they are both at Castle Rock productions. Unfortunately for my career, I told both Horn and Padnick at one time or another to go to hell. So, it's no surprise to me or them that you won't see my name associated with any Castle Rock projects.

There are times during my career that I look back on and say, "Oh, that was my bratty period." Sometimes I would get mad at people (like I did at the producers who replaced Norman Lear) but as I mentioned previously, more often than not it was *food*. While I was directing *One Day at a Time* I went through a period where I ate no meat. I came down one night before the show to have some dinner with the cast and crew and discovered that all that was left was meat. Specifically, the meat on the menu was roast beef, which from what I could tell by looking at it was so rare it still had a pulse. When the head caterer handed me the entree, I simply walked over to the garbage can and dumped the entire meal, plate and all, into the garbage can. That was my testiness at its best.

Sometimes, however, my testiness backfired and ended up costing me a job. Maybe it's because I'm short, but whenever I get into a fight I know that the only chance I have of winning is to talk fast enough to get myself out of trouble. One year I was doing a pilot for Norman Lear's company and at the end of the first day we went up to the producers' offices and they started to complain about the staging. Even though this was only our first day on the stage, they were already identifying problems.

The script was in terrible shape, but all the producers could talk about was the staging. Suddenly, I just couldn't take it any more. I said calmly, but with an obvious undercurrent of venom in my voice, "Maybe you should get somebody else to come in here and do this." I had thought that my threat would wake them up, but instead it got me fired. Within ten seconds they were on the phone hiring my replacement. It turned out for the best because I hated the pilot, but it served as a warning to me that I should pick my fights more carefully in the future.

There was one experience on *One Day at a Time* that I think summed up for me how desperately I was trying to connect to other people, but how, despite my best efforts, I was always coming up empty-handed. I used to try to share personal details about myself with the cast members so they would like me better. One day my daughter Leigh wrote a letter as a school assignment about what it was like to be adopted. It was something we had always talked openly about in our family, but in this letter Leigh was really sharing her feelings about the event with me for the first time.

Aside from Pat Harrington, Jr., I didn't stay in touch with many of the people from *One Day at a Time*, despite the fact that I directed the show for seven years (which for some directors is an entire career). I think the problem is this: On a studio soundstage the idea of anybody being part of a family for any long period of time is false. We all knew that we would be connected, employed, and working together for only as long as the network wanted us on the air and the production company wanted us in our parts. We could all be replaced. I think that sense of impending doom, the fear of never knowing when the show will end, always lurks somewhere inside of the dark walls of a soundstage.

There was one experience on *One Day at a Time* that I think summed up for me how desperately I was trying to connect to other people, but how, despite my best efforts, I was always coming up empty-handed. I used to try to share personal details about myself with the cast members so they would like me better. One day my daughter Leigh wrote a letter as a school assignment about what it was like to be adopted. It was something we had always talked openly about in our family, but in this letter Leigh was really sharing her feelings about the event with me for the first time.

I was very moved by the letter and was eager to share it with the other members of my sitcom "family." I decided to show the letter first to Bonnie Franklin. My relationship with her had always been a little strained because of tension with her personal manager, and I thought showing her my daughter's letter would extend a bridge to bring Bonnie and me closer. Unfortunately, my plan failed. After she read the letter, Bonnie just stared at me blankly with a look that said, "So, what?" Her lack of interest made me realize I had made a mistake. I took the letter back and folded it neatly into its envelope.

I thought I had found the perfect family on *One Day at a Time* but I was wrong. I did, however, find one "relative" who would remain with me. Her name is Pat Fischer and she was my secretary on *One Day at a Time*. Before long she was promoted to associate director and went on to do almost every taped show I've done since.

In the very old days when a director moved from series to series he would take his entire staff with him. But these days things are so pared down that you hope to take at least a few of your best people. With Pat I was able to develop a shorthand that saved time. Pat is the most loyal, talented assistant that anybody could ever have or wish for. And she's also probably one of the best friends I have in the world.

The house in Montana where I now live is filled with baby pictures of my grandson, Kyle. To a stranger the number of baby pictures would probably seem excessive. But aside from my children and Kyle, I don't have many other friends. I think I'm a good friend and I treasure the friends I have, but sometimes I wish I had more close relationships. Oddly enough, in Montana where I have only lived for a few years, I have a much better social support system than in Los Angeles, where I have lived for more than three decades. In Montana life may be a lot less sophisticated than Hollywood, but it's also a lot simpler and friendlier. I like it that way.

One of the things that has always amused me is when an actor leaves a successful television series with the explanation that he needs to "stretch himself." Pernell Roberts left TV's *Bonanza* and stretched himself out of about a zillion dollars. Bonnie Franklin traveled down a similar path. She had been starring in *One Day at a Time* for nine years when the network offered her a tenth season. She turned down CBS saying that she was going to return to Broadway where she belonged. Of course, since then she has made one tap dance cassette, and I'm probably one of the few who bought a copy. She left a successful series that paid her extremely well to go and stretch herself. Some actors simply don't recognize their good fortune until they've lost it.

After *One Day at a Time* I went on to direct several pilots and short-lived sitcoms such as *Harry's Battles* with Dick Van Dyke, *Sam* with Loretta Swit, and a series called *We Got It Made* that starred Teri Copley,

Tom Villard, and Matt McCoy. *We Got It Made,* an NBC series, was about two young New York bachelors who hired a sexy live-in maid. The series, patterned along the lines of *Three's Company,* was ultimately a forgettable one, and only lasted a season. But it did leave a lasting impression on me as a sitcom director.

We Got It Made was a series that I could point to and say tangibly, "Television is changing again." I remember the ratings were dropping and an executive from NBC said to me, "Does Teri have to wear a bra?" I thought that was one of the most horrendous things I'd ever heard. With thinking like that, it wasn't a surprise that the series was soon off the air. But I'll never forget that comment because it made me realize that network executives could be ludicrous as well as smart.

I went on to direct another series, this time for CBS, called *Charles in Charge* starring Scott Baio. I directed the pilot for the series. Later, although I didn't really get along with the show's producers, I stayed with the series because I liked working with Scott Baio.

Scott had a great regard for his parents, who were also his managers. He was not only fun on the set, but also a good guy off the set. He would listen to me and showed people the amount of respect they deserved and more so. Whenever I think about Scott I say to myself, "I'd work with Scott Baio again any day of the week." As an actor and as a person his manners were far beyond his years and I think that's why he's still working in this business today as a director.

It was while I was directing *Charles in Charge* that my heart once again gave me a wake-up call. Since my first heart surgery I had dramatically changed my diet and started exercising more. But in 1984, I had some pains in my legs. They were those same pains that I had felt before, shooting up through my body, as if searching for a place to strike. I knew I was in trouble again and needed to get help.

I went back east to see a childhood friend of mine, Dr. Mickey Mintz, and his son, Dr. Bruce Mintz. They checked my legs and decided to give me a full angiogram. Following the test results, they sent me back to Los Angeles, where I was seen by a cardiologist named Dr. Ronald Berez who had the bedside manner of a mortician. My children, who were understandably nervous about my condition, couldn't stand Dr. Berez. Although he did lack the usual social graces, I adored him. Berez was a brilliant technician and exactly who I needed in charge of my case.

While my first heart surgery occurred on my daughter Leigh's birthday, the date of my second heart surgery was also significant: March 2, 1984. It was the birthday of the man I had tried so hard to please and still tried daily to impress, even though he was dead. It was my father's birthday. I knew that I needed to survive this second surgery because I needed to get back to work to continue my efforts to try and make my dad proud. If I had died on his birthday, I'm sure he would have said, "Al did it on purpose to aggravate me."

8.

Another Marriage,
Another Heart Surgery,
and Some Bad Chicken Soup

I'm not a person who has ever had a lot of hobbies. I took up tennis when I moved to California, and I try to play three or four times a week for exercise. And, of course, I have my weekly poker game. It's not that outside things don't interest me, it is just that work always interested me more. Today I watch television shows like *Seinfeld* and *Ellen* more for good business than relaxation. Entertainment for entertainment's sake always made me feel like I was wasting my time. I'd rather be reading a script or spending some extra rehearsal time with an actor than dabbling in a hobby that wasn't going to get me anywhere as a director.

Someone once asked me if I traveled a lot and I said, "Not really," acting casually as if traveling never interested me. The truth is that I was never much of a traveler because getting on an airplane would take me too far away from the soundstage, which was my home. Traveling to shoot an episode of *The Love Boat* was safe because it was work. But in most other cases, if I couldn't be on a soundstage, then I couldn't work and then where would I be? A sitcom director without a soundstage is a man without a job. And that was one of my biggest fears.

I must admit that I enjoyed traveling to England a few times to see Wimbledon because of my interest in tennis; and I was fascinated by visits to Turkey, Israel, and China as part of my *Love Boat* directing assignment. (Israel was particularly memorable: While sightseeing we were shocked to hear orthodox Jews shouting "Doc" and "Gopher" as they recognized our stars.) But I'm not someone who likes to throw his toothbrush in a duffel bag and head off on a whim to any old point on the map. I'm much more of a planner. That's another reason why I love the house I built in Montana. It's a place to go to that is comfortable and familiar, yet just exotic enough for my tastes. In Montana I can jet ski, water ski, or ride in my speed boat right outside my front door. It sounds better than most vacation spots to me.

When I was directing sitcoms back-to-back, I didn't need to get on a plane to find my ideal destination either. It was right there on any studio soundstage. The crafts service table had plenty of food. There were more than enough beautiful women to look at. And there were dozens of men and women to talk to. Aside from the fact that the weather was usually pretty dreary on a soundstage, what more could anyone want in a job or a vacation? In some respects, I was like the traveler who keeps returning to the same city, the same hotel, and asking for the same room on the same floor year after year. I was never sure if I was as happy as the travel brochures said I should be, but I was always certain that I would go back next season to direct another episode.

■ ■ ■ ■ ■

One of my favorite TV series during the early 1970s was *The Flip Wilson Variety Show.* I had nothing to do with the series, but I enjoyed it because of Geraldine Jones, the sassy female character Flip played in weekly skits who had a jealous boyfriend named Killer. Geraldine made me laugh, and I thought Flip was an incredibly talented comedian. At that point I had never even met the man, but I imagined him to be very charming. Unfortunately, first-hand experience would soon prove me wrong.

When I got a call in 1985 to direct a series called *Charlie & Co.* starring Flip Wilson, I jumped at the opportunity because I was such a big fan. The series was not only being created as a vehicle for Flip, but also as the acting transition for singer Gladys Knight. I met with Gladys first and was quite impressed. She was one of those people you meet and say to yourself, "She comes from great stock." She had a wonderful sense of family values about her and seemed to have what it would take to move from singing into an acting career.

Backstage I became friends with Gladys's brother Bubba, who also was a member of her musical group, The Pips. Bubba usually hung around on the set and we would often spend time talking. We played tennis a few times together and became pretty good friends. He seemed very interested in watching me direct the series, and I was the kind of director who enjoyed it when others studied my methods. I thought that perhaps Bubba was taking some mental notes for a possible career in directing. I'm not sure if he ever did pursue it, but he always seemed like a very thoughtful man.

While Gladys and her brother Bubba impressed me, the star of the series did not. Flip revealed himself to be a pretty strange man. When we shot the pilot, the script called for a sentimental father-daughter scene between Flip and Fran Robinson, who played his fifteen-year-old on *Charlie & Co.* When we were rehearsing I told Flip that I thought it was important that he look Fran right in the eyes when he delivered his speech. He said he agreed but when we started to rehearse again I had to interrupt.

"Flip, I thought you said you were going to look her in the eyes?" I asked.

"Right," he said.

"Well, what's the problem?" I said.

"There's no problem. I am looking her in the eyes."

But there was a problem: He wasn't looking her in the eyes at all. He was looking around her, over her, and underneath her. He was looking everywhere but into her eyes. The fact that Flip refused to make eye contact should have been my first clue that something wasn't right. Flip's erratic concentration became more troublesome with each day.

Gladys was probably the first one to come to me and complain about Flip. She said he had trouble touching her. I remember one time they were supposed to be lying in bed as husband and wife discussing a family matter. The dialogue called for them to start warming up to each other, but it seemed that the warmer Gladys got, the colder Flip became. She said he recoiled from her touch and just refused to relate to her in any way. I tried to talk to Flip about it, but he didn't catch on. Other than bringing the problem out in the open, there was little else I could do.

Flip was also prone to mood swings. He vacillated between being a warm teddy bear and a cold fish. He could be friendly and loving in the morning, and irritable and angry by the afternoon. Another problem was that he never took the time to learn his lines. I remember being surprised that, despite his inconsistent behavior, he always managed to show up for work on time. I soon discovered that his on-time performance was due to proximity rather than effort. Flip would sometimes sleep on the stage in his dressing room overnight.

I probably wouldn't have felt so sad in retrospect about Flip's attitude, but just getting the show on the air was a minor miracle, and to see it turn into much less than it should have been is hard on everyone. For me there was, luckily, always another show, but for the majority of the cast, it was a severe blow. It meant no steady paycheck and no recognition, and it also meant having to go back to those tough auditions. One person can change a lot of lives.

I look back and think, "What could I have done better or more of?" I think, in my defense, that many celebrities are good actors, and they use the talents of their craft to hide their demons from the people they work with.

Flip's erratic behavior was a shame because *Charlie & Co.* had a lot going for it, including a young actor named Jaleel White. Jaleel played Flip's nine-year-old son and now stars in a series of his own called *Family Matters*. (His portrayal of Steve Urkel, the lovable nerd, has been making people laugh since 1989.) When I directed Jaleel on *Charlie & Co.* you could already tell he was a very bright kid with a supportive family. His father was a dentist, and his mother spent her days on the set looking after her son.

When the news came down from the network that *Charlie & Co.* had been canceled after only a single season, Jaleel cried right there on the spot. We hugged each other and I tried to tell him that there would be other shows, and hopefully better shows, ahead for his career. I haven't seen him in years, but from what I can gather from his recent television work, he's still one hell of a kid.

After *Charlie & Co.*, I directed a short-lived sitcom called *She's the Sheriff* with Suzanne Somers. She played a widow who took over her husband's job as sheriff of a small Nevada town after he died. The series and its plot lines were ultimately forgettable to me, except for one incident that happened on the set. We were in our first day of rehearsals when a studio page arrived unexpectedly on the set with a group of wealthy-looking people in tow. I was not happy to see them, especially because there had been no advance warning of the tour. I told the page it was inappropriate and that he would have to arrange another time for the visit. I didn't like surprises, especially when they occurred on my set when we were trying to work.

The next day I got a call from a studio executive who said, "Well Alan, when you do it, you really do it."

I had no idea what she was talking about.

"What happened?" I asked.

"Remember that group you threw off your set yesterday?" she asked. "It was lead by the Sultan of Brunei, a man we had been hoping to do business with. You threw the wealthiest man in the world off your set."

Needless to say I didn't win any points with the studio brass that week, but ultimately all was forgiven.

Like *She's the Sheriff*, most of the TV series I directed could fit pretty snugly into the traditional sitcom mold, but there was one that stands out in my mind as innovative and that was *It's Garry Shandling's Show*. The series was the precursor to Shandling's popular *Larry Sanders Show*. *It's Garry Shandling's Show* appeared on the Showtime and Fox networks, after allegedly being rejected by the three primary networks. The series featured a neurotic comic named Garry who often looked straight into the camera and spoke directly to the audience. He basically, as they say in show business, broke the "fourth wall of comedy" between fiction and real life.

As far as Garry went, he was one of the most self-centered human beings I've ever worked with, but he was also a very nice person. You usually don't find those two characteristics within the same body, but with Garry that was the case. He could be friendly, yet at times unpredictable and inexplicable. I remember one time we were filming a scene in front of the audience when the camera lights went off leaving Garry confused. He didn't know where to go next. So, he turned to me and yelled in a rather angry tone, "You take care of the cameras. I'll take

With Garry Shandling on the set of his series, *It's Garry Shandling's Show. Courtesy of Garry Shandling.*

care of the material." It was the only time he was ever unpleasant to me, but I never forgot it.

On the series I also worked with producer Alan Zweibel, who I think is one of the brightest and most talented writers in the business. Alan wrote for *Saturday Night Live* during its early days, and many of us on the set of *It's Garry Shandling's Show* encouraged Alan to share some of his hair-raising stories from that series. His memories, filled with names like John Belushi, Dan Aykroyd, and Gilda Radner, were endlessly entertaining to us.

On one episode of our series, Alan's friend Gilda Radner appeared as a guest star. To the best of my knowledge, her performance was her last on a television series because she died soon after, losing her noble battle with ovarian cancer. During rehearsals she would joke, "I'm going to the ladies' room and I'll be back in about two hours." From what I understand she was in constant pain and discomfort. Even though I

With producer Alan Zweibel and Red Buttons on the set of *It's Garry Shandling's Show. Courtesy of Alan Zweibel and Red Buttons.*

only directed Gilda in that one episode, I (like most of the people who met her) came away enchanted.

When I was with Gilda I didn't feel like I was with someone who was terminally ill, but rather in the presence of a fine human being. Since her death, Alan has written a book and an autobiographical stage play titled *Bunny, Bunny,* about some of the conversations he and Gilda shared. I read the book and loved it almost as much as I enjoyed working with the two of them.

The atmosphere on the set of *It's Garry Shandling's Show* was generally terrific, but I did sometimes feel an undercurrent of elitism as far as the humor went. I think it's the same kind of elitism that exists on programs such as *Seinfeld* and *The David Letterman Show,* where the philosophy is that only what comedians are currently serving up is funny. If it happened chronologically before the late 1980s, then the humor is

With guest star Gilda Radner and producer Alan Zweibel on the set of *It's Garry Shandling's Show.* This was one of Gilda's last appearances on television before she died of cancer. *Courtesy of Alan Zweibel.*

discounted by many of the people who work for and write on these shows. It's rather like comedy ageism. Many of these young comedians don't see how their careers evolved from those who came before them, people like Sid Caesar, Milton Berle, and Jack Benny.

I remember one afternoon I was sitting around a writers' table on *It's Garry Shandling's Show* and I mentioned the name Jimmy Durante. I got the strangest stares from the writers. Half of them were trying to figure out who Jimmy Durante was, and the other half were thinking, "Who cares about that dead guy?" It's a shame that comedy elitism exists because I think someday a sitcom might benefit from having a mixed writing staff—with people in their sixties and people in their thirties. Unfortunately, no one has been able to make it work yet. These days if a show does hire an older writer, they usually end up patronizing him or ignoring him completely.

I was nominated for an Emmy award for an episode of *It's Garry Shandling's Show* that I directed. This time (marking my fourth nomination) I did not win. But I did earn two ACE awards for the series (ACE awards recognize cable programs). Winning the ACE awards was ironic because when I was first hired to direct the series I was a little snobbish. It felt like I was being sent down to the minor leagues because it was cable and not network television. I soon discovered that what is happening on cable is often more exciting and groundbreaking than on the networks. It proved to be a real boon to my career.

Because *It's Garry Shandling's Show* broke the fourth wall of comedy, I also had to learn a whole new set of directing rules. For example, I had to shoot a set so that you saw it was a set instead of a real-life living room. The premise was to reveal, rather than disguise or hide, the realistic and unique aspects of a soundstage. I also had to set up for the shots where Garry talked directly to the camera. I'd never had to deal with anything like that before and for that reason the series was educational for me.

The success of the series was largely due to Garry and his ability to be creative as well as funny. When *It's Garry Shandling's Show* went off the air, Garry didn't waste any time in plotting his return. His next great idea was *The Larry Sanders Show,* a talk-show spoof. I think even if Garry wasn't a great performer, he could be equally successful if he stuck with writing, producing, or directing.

I've been talking a lot about my professional life and sharing little about my private life because basically, since divorcing my first wife, Ann, in 1970, there was very little to talk about during the 1980s. If I wasn't working, I was spending time with my daughters or preparing for my next directing job. There wasn't a lot of extra time to spend concentrating on dating. Perhaps my lack of a personal life is one of the reasons why I so impulsively and unexpectedly married my second wife in 1987.

I had been single for more than seventeen years and was sitting on the deck of my house in Malibu when I saw an incredible pair of breasts walking toward me. That's the only way I can explain it. The large breasts belonged to a woman named Barbara Gilbert, whom I'd known on and off over the years. She had already been married a number of times. The first time was to Paul Gilbert, who was a brilliant physical comedian. But even today, Barbara is well known in Los Angeles not for her marriages, but for her talented children. She is the mother of actresses Melissa Gilbert (*Little House on the Prairie*) and Sara Gilbert (*Roseanne*), and actor Jonathan Gilbert (who also appeared on *Little House on the Prairie*).

Barbara and I were married three months to the day after I saw her walking along the beach. Unfortunately, thirteen weeks after we said "I do," we said "I quit" and got divorced. The story reminds me of actor Tim Conway who had personalized car license plates that read "13 Weeks" because he never had a TV series that lasted more than thirteen weeks. The networks decided that Tim's shows weren't working in that amount of time, and Barbara and I came to the same conclusion about our marriage.

I can't really offer much insight into my marriage to Barbara except to say that although it was brief, it was still painful to realize we had made such a mistake. I probably jumped in before I was ready, and later realized that Barbara and I weren't in any way the soul mates we were looking for. I should have known we were in trouble when we went to Santa Monica to take out our marriage license. Barbara wouldn't let me see the license because it had her age on it. I had no idea how old this lady was whom I was about to make my wife. Six weeks after our divorce was final, she got married again, which I don't think made anyone who knew her bat an eye.

Oddly enough, her daughter Sara was the person I felt closest to in the family. I never met her son and I always found Melissa to be kind of a flighty girl. Sara and I got along great. She was only twelve years old when I married her mother, but she was a very bright and perceptive little girl. Shortly after Barbara and I got divorced, I got a call from Sara. She said, "I got a series! I got on a TV series!"

Sara had done some performing before, but I had no idea she was auditioning for a series.

"What's the series?" I asked.

"It's a pilot called *Roseanne*."

"Who's Roseanne?"

"The stand-up comedian, Roseanne Barr. You know . . ."

"I don't know her, but I've heard of her. It sounds great," I said.

I was tickled that Sara felt close to me and wanted to share the good news.

Around the same time Sara was cast as Darlene Conner on *Roseanne*, I was hired to direct a vehicle for another stand-up comedian, Jackie Mason. The series was called *Chicken Soup*, and unfortunately it tops my list as the worst and most unpleasant sitcom to direct of all-time. My disagreeable experience on *Chicken Soup* was far worse than even the tension of *Laverne & Shirley* or the embarrassment of *Me and the Chimp*.

Sara and I were filming on the same studio lot and sometimes I would go and visit her or she would stop in and see me. I was delighted with Sara's success as an actress and the fact that later she took time off from *Roseanne* to attend Yale University. It didn't surprise me that she was able to juggle a TV series and a college education because you could always tell she was a kid who was going to go far in life.

Other than visiting Sara, however, there wasn't much else to rave about in directing *Chicken Soup*. Jackie Mason was one of the most un-likeable people I've ever met and a royal pain to work with. He wore the same clothes every day and was extremely unclean in his appearance and his mouth. Lynn Redgrave played his co-star and I always felt sorry that she had to work opposite Jackie. Whenever the script called for her to kiss him, I wanted to gag. Lynn did everything she could to try and make Jackie feel at ease, but her professional efforts were simply lost on him.

I remember he'd go around to members of the crew saying, "Are you Jewish? Are you Jewish?"

I finally went up and confronted him.

"Jackie, you really should stop doing that," I said.

"How come?"

"It makes the crew uncomfortable," I said.

"Why? Are you ashamed of being Jewish?" he asked.

"No. I'm not ashamed. I just don't think it's any of your business what religion people are," I said.

When ABC canceled *Chicken Soup* after only two months on the air, I think most of us were not surprised, and some of us were even elated by the news. Although sad to be out of work, most of us were happy that we wouldn't have to work with Jackie any more. He could go bother somebody else.

On most shows, particularly situation comedies, the behavior of the cast comes from above, in other words, from the star. Unlike the case of *Chicken Soup*, on the set of *Murphy Brown*, star Candice Bergen set an exemplary standard for others to follow. The cast of *Murphy Brown*, which when I directed it included Charles Kimbrough, Joe Regalbuto, Faith Ford, and Grant Shaud, was a very professional group. Candice was the boss and it was not by accident that those who worked for her honored her requirement for precision and dedication.

Because the playtime in her life was reserved for her young daughter Chloe, Candice always came to the set ready to work. If the schedule said rehearsal was supposed to begin at ten in the morning, then she wanted everyone there at ten o'clock sharp with scripts in hand. If the schedule said we were supposed to break for lunch from one to two P.M., she wanted everyone back by two o'clock on the nose. She didn't want anyone wasting even a second of her time, and if you did you heard about it.

One day everyone straggled back from lunch a little late and we didn't start rehearsal until 2:30 P.M., although we had been scheduled to resume at 2:00 P.M. Candice, who was back right on time, turned to the first assistant director and registered her complaint. "If I'd known that everyone was going to be late, then I would have had time to attend a parent meeting at my daughter's school," Candice said. "So, if we are going to be back at two o'clock, let's make sure we're back at two. Okay?"

And that's the way it was. There was never a lot of visiting among actors in between scenes either. It was strictly business. Candice liked to start off the week reading the script out loud around a table with the cast sitting down. Then we would get up on our feet and rehearse each scene a few times until she and I were satisfied. Then we'd go on to the next scene and after working for an hour or so we'd take a five- or ten-minute break. During the break, Candice would go into her dressing room and take care of personal business.

Overall I enjoyed directing *Murphy Brown* and found Candice to be a delightful person. I suppose by the way I've described her rigid work habits that "delightful" sounds like hyperbole, but she really was a lot of fun to be around. Because of her work ethic, things ran so smoothly that we could all afford to have fun once in a while. The rest of the cast was usually on time, knew their lines, and was able to make helpful contributions to the staging process of the series.

The way that Candice influenced her cast reminds me of the way Dick Van Dyke dictated the tone on his series, and later Mary Tyler Moore did on the sitcom that carried her name. Everybody knew that Candice was not the type of star who wanted to be shooting until midnight on show night. She wanted to get home to her daughter. We would often pre-film some of the tougher scenes before the audience arrived. That way we could usually be headed home on Friday night by nine-thirty or ten o'clock. It was a respectable hour to finish a show and that's exactly the way Candice liked it.

▼ ▬ ▬ ▬ ▲

After two heart surgeries, I had become an expert at recognizing when my heart was in trouble and in 1988, my heart was in trouble again. Like the other two times, the pain started in my jaw. I returned to cardiologist Dr. Berez who confirmed my suspicion that I needed additional heart surgery. Only this time we ran into a problem: There weren't any veins left in my legs to perform another bypass.

So, they had to take the mammary artery in my chest and use that instead. If that hadn't worked, I don't know what they would have done, but I don't like to think about that. The surgery took place on my fifty-ninth birthday, July 23, and although it was deemed a success, the memories of three heart surgeries had started to take their toll on my life and the lives of my daughters. We had ridden the same roller coaster of fear, worry, and stress three times together and by the end of the third ride I think we were all pretty exhausted.

The worst part of the three operations was the fact that my children had to sit in a hospital corridor waiting to see if their daddy lived or died. Before the last operation I called Dru and Leigh into my hospital room and said, "If anything goes wrong, like I fall off the table or they hit me in the head with a broom or whatever, I want to see real mourning. I want crying and thrashing around on the floor from both of you. But I only want you to cry for half an hour. Then, take a deep breath and realize that nobody owed me anything and that I had the best life I could have had because I shared it with you guys."

Then I asked the girls to put their hands on me. They stood on either side of my hospital bed and laid their hands on my shoulders. I swear at that instant I felt their energy and love coming through me. Of course, at that same moment, my I.V. full of drugs began to hit me, and I was getting more stoned with each second. It was the most relaxed feeling I've ever had in my life. It was marvelous.

I remember later when I saw the doctor I said through the clouds of my drug haze, "Do you want to crack my chest open? Go ahead. Take your best shot." He did. And thanks to the doctors and the energy that I felt from my daughters, I made it through the surgery and continue to be in good shape today. I can't imagine going through what I have gone through without my daughters. They are literally the world to me and I cherish my relationship with them each day.

Late in the 1980s I was approached about directing a series for NBC called *A Family for Joe*. The series starred the great screen actor Robert Mitchum as a homeless man adopted by four upper-middle-class orphans to pose as their dad. Although Mitchum was one of the most famous movie stars of all time, his turn at television was not as successful.

From what I could gather, Mitchum had saved quite a bit of money from his movie career, but that money had been swindled by his business manager. So he had to go back to work as quickly as possible to try and recoup his losses. He started doing television commercials (one particularly embarrassing one was for meat) and then jumped at the chance when the NBC series came up. I have to admit that although Mitchum did the best he could with his lines, the scripts were terribly written from start to finish.

Despite the problematic series, Mitchum is a man I respect enormously. I think because I admired him so much, I was always a little sad that he had to return to work because of his financial problems. He's an actor who shouldn't have had to work unless he wanted to. The irony of his plight was never lost on the cast and crew of *A Family for Joe*. Sometimes we'd be rehearsing a scene and he'd beguile us with fascinating stories from his film career. He'd be standing there beside me saying, "It's 1954. I'm with Jane Russell on the set of *Macao* . . ." At least nobody could ever take his incredible body of work away from him.

It's noteworthy to mention that *A Family for Joe* also included a young actress named Juliette Lewis, who played one of the kids who adopted Mitchum. At the time, I didn't think Juliette was a very good actress, and I doubted that she would ever make it. Although her NBC audition had been excellent, she was miserable on the set. She spent a lot of time crying and would complain openly about how unhappy she was. She would say crazy things like, "I don't want to do this series. I want to work with De Niro." I remember thinking to myself, "Sure you'll work with De Niro." And of course later she proved me wrong by working not only with Robert De Niro (in *Cape Fear*), but also with Woody Allen (in *Husbands and Wives*) and Oliver Stone (in *Natural Born Killers*).

It was during *A Family for Joe* that I took another try at the dating game. I started seeing a woman named Roxanne, who'd been a model earlier in life and had found her way into television production. I met her when she worked for Bill D'Angelo, whom I had worked with on *Love, American Style* and had teamed up with again on *A Family for Joe*. Roxanne was Bill's executive assistant.

We started to go out, and I remember our first date was to see *Phantom of the Opera*. Then we began to see each other regularly, eventually spending weekends together. She'd come out to my house in Malibu and stay as long as she liked, even leaving some of her clothes there. She was an extremely charming woman and together we had a very uninhibited sex life, which was unusual for me. After two divorces, I was a man with a lot of relationship baggage, but Roxanne didn't make me feel that way.

We had dinners. We traveled to London to see Wimbledon. And we enjoyed being together. And then, all of the sudden, it fell apart. Looking back I suppose that I realized that I was enjoying myself too much and I choked. It ended when a woman whom I had known years before called and asked if I would be her date at a wedding. I said, "Sure. Why not?" When Roxanne found out, she was furious and said she was coming by the next day to pick up her clothes. Later we tried to talk it out, but it didn't work. There was no point. Perhaps I was too cocky at that stage in my life to commit to another woman. I didn't even put up much of a fight to save the relationship.

Years later I began to regret the breakup and wished things hadn't ended so badly. I figured that she probably would have given me a second chance, but I would have messed that up too. I was frightened. I think about Roxanne a lot. The last time I spoke with her she said she was living with someone and was very happy. She said the new relationship was working because there was no pressure. I thought that was a rather strange thing to say because I didn't realize there had ever been any pressure on our relationship. But I guess I was wrong.

Following my breakup with Roxanne, if someone had told me that I would soon be married for the third time, I would have said, "No.

That's not right. That's not the way to do it." But that's exactly what I did. In 1990 I met a woman named Aja who became my third wife. Like the previous marriages, this one also ended in divorce. The breakup with Aja would be the messiest and most painful for me. It was so distracting that I even allowed it to penetrate the armor of my career, an unforgivable sin in the past. But boy did this lady get to me.

9.

Breaking Up with Murphy Brown, Coach, and My Third Wife

If I had to pinpoint one characteristic that has made me a good director over the years I think, more than my technical skill, it has been my personality. My temperament is easygoing and when I walk into a room my inclination is to try and make people laugh to ease the tension. That's the way I was as a little boy, and that's the way I still am today at the age of sixty-eight. When I meet someone new of any age, I immediately want to find something in common with them, or at least something in common to laugh about.

My emphasis on humor is one of the reasons that I've always gotten along with actors. Aside from the fact that I respect, admire, and appreciate their talent, most actors have said they liked working with me because I wasn't threatening. Many television actors are surrounded in their daily lives by people who want things from them. Their agents want a commission. Their fans want an autograph. Their relatives want a job. The role of an actor is in itself a job that comes under assault every day. So, my goal was always to help actors give their best performance possible without taking anything away. I didn't want them to leave the set feeling anything more than the pride that we had all completed an episode we could be proud of (or at the very least an episode we had a lot of fun putting together).

I always tried to make an actor feel comfortable from the moment he walked on the set. Any series is made up of some actors who have worked a lot and some who may have never set foot on a sound-stage before. For any newcomer the experience can be daunting, and even for some television veterans it can be scary. The bottom line was that I pledged never to force an actor to do anything he didn't want to do. I positioned myself as an ally from the moment we all sat around the table for the first reading of the script until after shooting the show when we all got into our cars to drive home. I was on the actor's side.

I used to say that one thing that may have made me a little better than the next guy when it came to directing was that I could make an actor feel so safe that he would be willing to try things for me that he might have been too afraid to risk with someone else. If he tried an experiment and it bombed, then I would usually make fun of him to try and cushion the blow. I would then encourage him to try something else. I was most pleased when an actor stared me down, with a face sweating in determination, and said, "Okay. You don't like that, then what do you think of this?"

Striving for the right combination of comfort and humor was never as important as it was when I signed on to direct *Murphy Brown*. I remember when I started directing the series, the cast gave me a great amount of respect right off the bat because I had already directed many episodes of *Coach*, another top-rated sitcom. One day the *Murphy Brown* cast started to make a big fuss over me, boasting that they had "stolen" me away from the cast of *Coach*. Someone stood up and said, "We are so proud to have Alan Rafkin here this week." I then rose to my feet and said, "Thank you. It all started for me back in the late 1960s . . ." Everybody laughed because they knew that I never was one to take myself seriously for very long.

So, that's what I do and what I do well: I make actors feel safe and secure enough to do their job. Unfortunately, something would occur in the early 1990s that would interfere with the way I was doing my job. I had always prided myself on the fact that I could be a workaholic and still have some semblance of a life away from the set. I thought I had it all in balance until I married for the third time. The union was a disaster from start to finish. I can't help but look back on it as a major distraction from my professional life, and one of the all-time painful experiences in my personal life.

■ ▬ ▬ ▬ ▲

In the early 1990s my friend and former college roommate Marshall Gelfand and his wife, Judy, fixed me up with a woman named Aja Rodas. Originally from Finland, she worked as a sales woman at Neiman Marcus in Beverly Hills and also had been divorced twice. The first night I met Aja was at a dinner party at my house. When I opened the door to welcome her I was pleasantly surprised to see a short and stunning-looking blonde. She was dressed in exactly what I like to see a woman wear—a men's white shirt, blue blazer, jeans, white socks, and loafers. I stood at the door so long smiling that I almost forgot to ask her in. Six months later we were married.

The marriage, which lasted from 1992 until 1994, was wrong from day one. We did, however, build a beautiful house in Montana, and for that reason I will always be thankful. I never would have even gone to Montana if it hadn't been for Aja. Shortly before we were married we were thinking of buying some property, and Aja suggested that we check out Montana. Before her department store days Aja had been a stewardess for Pan Am, and a former stewardess friend of hers lived in Montana with her husband.

So, we traveled to Montana and stayed with Aja's friend in a small town called Rollins. The first morning I woke up and looked out the window to see three feet of snow on the ground. It was snowing so badly that you couldn't even drive a car. I said to myself, "There's no God damned way I'm ever going to buy a piece of land up here." But that afternoon, Aja and I bought the property next door.

What happened? I fell in love with Montana. The property next door was owned by a woman named Mabel Chester who had recently passed away. At one time Mabel had grown twenty-seven varieties of lilacs on her land. She had lived there for more than fifty years and had planted a blue spruce in the front yard the day she moved into the house. I thought that tree was one of the most gorgeous things I had ever seen. When I then realized that I had the opportunity to buy such a magnificent piece of land, it was too good to pass up.

The property had two acres and 200 feet of waterfront attached to it. Aja and I bought the land, tore down Mabel's small cabin, and built a house of our own on the land. I thought our future in Montana would resemble *On Golden Pond*, with us living out our retirements together sitting in rocking chairs on the porch. Well, I still may do that, but Aja most certainly won't be sitting beside me. I'd be happy if she never set foot in the state of Montana again. (I got the house in the divorce settlement, thanks to my business manager, Marshall Gelfand.)

The problem started when I was lying in my bed in Montana sick with pneumonia. A doctor looked at me and said that I wasn't sick enough to go to the hospital, but I needed to take it easy in bed. That's where I was when Aja said that she and a neighbor wanted to take out our power boat. She said the neighbor told her that our boat had been idle for too long and it needed to have its engine blown out. I said go ahead and then watched from my bed as my wife and another man rode off in the power boat that I had paid for with my television residuals. There I was coughing and hacking my brains out as I watched Aja sail away from me both literally and figuratively.

I soon heard that my wife and the neighbor were allegedly having an affair. It wasn't a difficult mystery to solve; news of that kind travels as fast in Rollins as it would if we lived in Mayberry. I was a cuckold. It's one thing to be a cuckold in a city the size of Los Angeles. But it's far worse to have it done to you when you are living in a town of 200 by a guy who lives less than 250 yards down the lane. There's no place to hide and no place to run. You simply have to face facts and try and hold your head as high as you can without letting the pain show. I had worked with actors long enough to direct myself this time.

Over the years it seems that I've been able to handle most everything that I've been hit with except deception. I've never had any use for it in my career or my personal life. Aja and I were at a dinner party one night in Montana when I found out about the alleged affair. I told her I was leaving, effective immediately. In her typical fashion she said, "You can't. We're hosting a dinner party tomorrow night." All she cared about was looking bad. I said, "No. It's over. You have a dinner party. I'm outta here." And that's how I left her.

Realizing that I had failed at my third trip to the altar hurt a lot. I had tried to be a good friend to her as well as a good husband, but the relationship was doomed from the start. We wanted different things out of life and we were too smitten with each other in the beginning to realize it. I've never considered myself to be the easiest person to get along with, but Aja revealed herself to be truly unkind. So for a third time, marriage was not to be what I had longed for all my life.

The year that I broke up with Aja was, ironically, one of my most successful years as a sitcom director. I was shooting ten episodes of *Murphy Brown* that season and eleven episodes of *Coach*. I remember thinking to myself, "Here I am directing two top-rated shows. I should be feeling pretty good about myself. Why am I feeling so terrible?" In the past I had always been able to hide inside my career, but the failure of the marriage tore me apart. There I was at sixty-three years old, alone again.

I remember times on the set of *Murphy Brown* when we'd break from rehearsal and I'd steal a quick moment to call Aja. I had a sick need to keep calling her even after we had broken up. Inevitably I'd hang up the phone in tears, having to return to the group and resume rehearsal. At the time I thought I was hiding my anxiety and tension over the breakup quite well, but it was more apparent than I thought. One time when I was obsessing over the divorce I snapped at one of the actors during a rehearsal and made a sarcastic remark about women in general. Candice Bergen fixed a tight gaze on me and said sarcastically, "Well, that's a nice attitude to bring to the set." The trauma and hurt I was feeling were too intense to hide behind my job. I was a wounded man whether I liked it or not.

After directing *Murphy Brown* for two seasons, I was not asked back for a third season. I was shocked at the time. But, looking back, I obviously had allowed my personal problems, for the first time in my career, to affect my professional life. My reaction to the divorce ended up causing irreversible damage to my relationship with Candice. When she saw how much energy I was expending on my divorce, Candice lost confidence in me as a director. That's when she decided not to hire me back and instead handed me my walking papers.

I can't hold anything against Candice for not asking me back, because ultimately it was her show and her decision to make. But I had loved directing *Murphy Brown* and thought I had been doing some good work with the cast. I think not being asked back was the first time that I realized my directing career was not going to go on forever. Someday there would come a time when it would end, and nobody would want me back. The thought that my career was not eternal scared me. To this day I admire Candice as an actress, and I hope that some day we will have the opportunity to sit down and talk. At the time, I didn't dare approach the issue. It was time for me to move on.

After parting with the cast and crew of *Murphy Brown*, I spent more time at my house in Montana. I found the time away from the smog of Los Angeles and the headaches of Hollywood was therapeutic. My visits evolved into longer stays, usually from April through September. Then, I would return to my condominium in Los Angeles on Wilshire Boulevard and set myself up for the upcoming television season. When I was in California I worked; when in Montana I relaxed. I would play poker in Montana maybe once or twice a week and also arranged a weekly tennis match with a few buddies. I was living two lives in two different states with two separate sets of friends, but I had few complaints.

My big activity in Montana remains going to town to get my mail at the local post office. It's a ritual I relish. It's not that I always get exciting mail, rather it's the pilgrimage that I enjoy. Sometimes when I go into town in the morning I see a group of men gathered together drinking from coffee mugs with their names on them. They sit around, talk, and sip their caffeine. I often think to myself that I could become a part of their coffee klatch. I'm not sure that we all share the same views on politics and guns, but the men are always very gracious to me when they see me walk in to get my mail.

One of the best things about Montana is that it makes me feel less hyper. In Los Angeles I always feel like I have to run in order to squeeze in all the things I want to accomplish. In Montana I'm ruled by a slower pace. One of my neighbors is a doctor who also loves to act. Sometimes we gather in my house and do play readings with the doctor and some of the other amateur actors in town. For more organized entertainment, we have a summer theater in Big Fork, which is thirty minutes away; and there are thankfully a lot of movies and books on my shelves to watch and read.

The only real complaint that I have about Montana is the food. When you go to eat at a restaurant, it's not unusual to find sixteen different kinds of meat on the menu ranging from beef to buffalo to venison. Way down at the bottom of the menu in very small print you might find a chicken dish. And if you dare to ask your waiter about fish, don't expect anything that hasn't spent time in a freezer. For a man like myself who has had three heart surgeries, living in a place overrun with beef is often a trial. But I watch my cholesterol and try to do the best I can. Most of my meals are eaten at home where I design the menu myself.

One of the things that I love about Montana is that it's a true luxury for me to spend time there. I can drive down I-93 at ninety miles an hour if I want to. I love it because it is so different from Los Angeles. Many of my friends from Hollywood still can't believe that I built a house in Montana. Some friends ask me curiously, "What do you do up there?" I take secret joy in the fact that I can't explain it. I simply have to live it.

Despite my increasing time in Montana, my industry ties to Los Angeles were stronger than ever in the early 1990s. I signed on to direct the comedy series *Coach*, which was then in the middle of its second

With the cast of *Coach. Moving clockwise:* Jerry Van Dyke, me, Clare Carey, Craig T. Nelson, Shelley Fabares, Georgia Engel, Ken Kimmins, and Bill Fagerbakke. *Copyright © by Universal City Studios, Inc.*

season on ABC. The sitcom starred Craig T. Nelson, Jerry Van Dyke, and Shelley Fabares. The scripts focused on the life of a college football coach and the antics of his bumbling team. I remember at the beginning of my first season with the show, Craig welcomed everyone back and said, in essence, that he thrived on trouble and liked it when the pot was boiling. At the time I thought he was kidding, but I would soon find out he was not.

To say the series was in turmoil and chaos when I arrived is an understatement. The cast and crew had already chewed through at least a dozen directors for a variety of reasons ranging from insufficient skills to personality conflicts. I came onboard, directed a few episodes, and wasn't quite sure what to expect next. Then, *Coach* creator and executive producer, Barry Kemp, asked me to direct all of the following season. I decided that it was a pleasant enough show and I might like to stick around for a while. But I knew the tide could turn at any moment, so I had to be prepared for anything.

In the beginning, I really enjoyed directing *Coach*. One of my favorite things about the series was renewing my friendship with actress Shelley Fabares. I had loved Shelley since I directed her on *The Donna Reed Show* during the early 1960s. I had worked with her again in the early 1980s on *One Day at a Time*, when she played Bonnie Franklin's nemesis turned business partner in a recurring role. *Coach* represented a chance for me to work closely again with Shelley and that thrilled me.

Another friendly face on the set of *Coach* was comedian Jerry Van Dyke, who played the show's assistant coach, Luther Van Dam. Jerry still remains a close friend (and one of my friends who finds it odd that I like to spend so much time in Montana). In my book, he is one of the funniest comedians around. If you go to see Jerry perform in a nightclub, you should go to the bathroom before the show starts or you'll need to soon. He's simply hysterical. I also think he's underrated as an actor. He brought so much of his own talent and perspective to his character on *Coach*, but I don't think he ever received enough recognition for a job well done.

While I was directing *Coach*, the cast and crew treated me very well, especially in the beginning. Many people on the series confided in me that before I arrived they felt like they were employed on a sinking ship. Now that I was directing, however, they felt like the ship was on a straight and steady course. It was a wonderful compliment for any director to hear, especially one who had been with the series for such a short time. The cast and crew also had an allegiance to the show that made it a pleasure to direct them. No matter what the ratings were, they went doggedly about their work. There would, however, be rough waters ahead for both me and the cast and crew. The turbulence would come from none other than the star of the show, Craig T. Nelson.

▗▄▄▄▄▄▄▄▄

I always believed that Craig was a wonderful actor, but unfortunately his temperament didn't live up to his talent. He became increasingly difficult to work with because of his unpredictable attitude and mood swings. I began to carefully look for clues to try and anticipate his behavior. If I said, "Good morning, Craig," and he came back with, "Hey man, how's it going?" then I knew it was going to be a good day.

If, however, he responded with, "I don't want to be here," or simply walked right by me, then I knew I had to watch out. Trouble was on its way.

The first few seasons we lived with Craig's attitude for the good of the series. But later on, Craig became the kind of actor I classify as "undirectable." He professed that he knew his character better than anybody else, and he was willing to fight with anyone who said anything different. All of my stage suggestions and directions were met with patronizing comments and irritated glances from Craig. In addition, he started to become inconsiderate and unpleasant to other members of the cast and crew. (Ironically, if he did another project like a movie-of-the-week, he behaved much better and accepted direction. It was only on the set of *Coach* that he insisted on running things his way or not at all.)

The examples are numerous, but I remember that cigarette smoking was a major point of contention on *Coach*. Like most other soundstages, the *Coach* stage was designated "No Smoking." Craig, however, considered himself to be above the rules. He would light up a cigarette whenever he wanted (which increasingly seemed to be more often than not). Instead of trying to hide his transgression, he flaunted it. One day some of the crew members wanted to know why they couldn't smoke too. The assistant director told them, "This is not a democracy. Craig will smoke if he wants to because this is his show." Period. No more discussion.

I thought that Craig probably had a lot of demons rambling around inside of him because he always seemed so troubled. He could be sweet one minute and sour the next. He didn't seem to get the same joy and excitement out of show night that other actors did. His highs never balanced out his lows. Sometimes he would arrive for show night and still hadn't taken the time to learn his lines. He was like a man diving off a pier into cold water. He'd throw caution to the wind and somehow come up with a fine performance, despite his antagonistic attitude and lack of preparation.

Unfortunately, the more control Craig demanded, the more control I gave him. It got to the point where I was rendered completely powerless as a director, and I was partially to blame. If I didn't like something that Craig was doing in a scene, I very often would be too fearful to yell "Cut!" because I knew he would turn around and say, "What the fuck is wrong?" So I would let him do the scene once his way. Then under false pretenses I would find some reason to do the scene again. Only the second time, I would try and slip Craig a suggestion or two. Sometimes he would still scream at me, but apologize to me later in private out of the crew's earshot. (I thought that was rather cowardly.)

I can remember during my early days on *Coach* when producer Barry Kemp would come out on the stage after a show night and thank everyone. Then he would add "and a big thank you to our director Alan Rafkin who has again led us through a very tumultuous week to arrive at another wonderful ending." Ironically, today Barry wouldn't hire me if I were the last director on earth. My tenure with *Coach* ended badly. We all soon came to the conclusion that *Coach* didn't need a director. What the series need was a "yes man" for Craig. We all also knew that a "yes man" certainly came a lot cheaper than me.

By the time I was ready to leave *Coach,* even the producer was coming to blows with his star. One of the last things I remember is the day that Craig made a derogatory remark about one of the writers. Barry quickly jumped to the writer's defense. Their argument escalated to the point where they looked at each other with expressions that read, "words are no longer enough. It's time to use our fists." I watched an eighty-pound script girl crawl under her desk to protect herself from the possible bloodshed as the two men headed outside. A few minutes later Barry marched back in with Craig trailing behind him like a puppy. That's when I knew definitively that it was time to leave. The *Coach* set was no longer a place for a comedy director. It was time for me to move on once again.

I signed on to direct a new NBC series called *Hope and Gloria* about two neighbors in a Pittsburgh apartment building who become friends. The series starred Cynthia Stevenson, Jessica Lundy, and Alan Thicke. At the time, many people praised the talent of Cynthia, who is a fine young comedian, but I also thought Jessica was wonderful. I directed her as if she were a diamond in the rough. She certainly didn't have the comedy experience that Cynthia had, but Jessica had the potential to go places. Unfortunately, Jessica spent the majority of her time on the set of *Hope and Gloria* being misunderstood.

Jessica used to ask the writers and producers a lot of questions. They began to resent her constant queries and, in my opinion, they started to mistreat her as an actress. Their attitude was that she should just do the show as written, and stop asking so many questions about the script. She was an actress, not a puppet, and I think they may have been looking for more of the latter. Maybe Jessica didn't always ask her questions with the perfect amount of grace, but I think that stemmed from her own frustration and inexperience as the star of a network series.

What I thought the producers didn't understand was that deep down Jessica really did have a comedic soul. Instead of cultivating her talent, they beat her up for it. One day the producers sat me down to talk about a problem.

"Tell Jessica to stop mugging," they said.

"What does that mean?" I asked.

"Mugging. She's mugging too much for the camera," they said.

"That's hardly a constructive note," I said, frustrated by the fact that they were once again misunderstanding her.

I didn't know what to do with their comment, so I decided to be direct. Like a schmuck I went up to Jessica and said, "The producers want you to stop mugging for the camera."

Jessica burst into tears. She was upset because they weren't specific. She wanted to know examples of when they thought she was "mugging," but I couldn't give her any. I could only try and console her.

"Don't cry," I said. "It's a stupid note and I never should have told you. It makes no sense at all. They just don't understand you."

It took me a long time to regain Jessica's confidence, and eventually she came back stronger than ever. But for the run of the series, *Hope and Gloria* was just never the nurturing place it should have been for Jessica. Her talent deserves better and I hope some day she finds a series more conducive to her style of acting.

Cynthia, on the other hand, was treated with a lot more respect on the series because she played by the producers' rules. She was a terrific actress and a pleasure to direct. She is one of those actresses whose positive and productive attitude is contagious. She always came to work prepared and wearing a smile. It didn't matter what happened yesterday, or an hour ago, or ten minutes ago; Cynthia always was there ready to rehearse. She was also resilient. If we got a revised script back from the writers and it was as awful as the original, Cynthia still gave it everything she had. I would love to work with her again.

Alan Thicke also appeared on *Hope and Gloria*. Much to everyone's surprise and pleasure, he was a big success. I thought he was wonderful as Dennis Dupree, the dim-witted talk show host. As an actor on the series, Alan was always creative and made his suggestions like a gentleman. Everyone knew him to be a very social animal, always going off to host celebrity tennis tournaments and judge beauty contests. He even married a former Miss World. The best thing about working with Alan is that he always seems to be enjoying life and having a great time at whatever he's doing.

When people find out that I've been a sitcom director for close to forty years, many of them ask me how television has changed. The largest change that I have noticed is in the steady redistribution of authority. For example, during the 1970s I would direct a run-through and then turn around and get notes from one person—a Norman Lear, a Bob Ross, a Carl Reiner, or another executive producer of that caliber. There would be one person to talk to, and he and I would discuss what worked and what didn't. Today, I turn around and instead of facing one person, I am faced with more than a dozen people.

On any TV series today there can be nine or ten producers. Many of the writers now receive producing credit, and then there is the ever-expanding parade of executive producers, producers, associate producers, and on and on. The gaggle of producers huddle together and then turn around to the director and say, "We think . . ." Such production by committee often leaves the director out in the cold.

The hardest part for me is that many producers seem so willing to compromise rather than put in the hard work to make episodes as strong as they can be. For example, sometimes because of scheduling I'm forced to show the producers a scene that I know is not working yet. In the old days, a producer might help me tinker with a scene that was funny, but not quite perfect. Today, more often than not, they say, "Fine. Let's move on." They settle too quickly to get an episode finished as fast as they can. No matter how hard I try, I still can't get used to the complacency. When I know something isn't fine, it's hard for me just to move on.

I suppose I was spoiled as a director when I worked with some of the great producers during the 1970s. I remember an experience on *Rhoda* when there was a scene that just wasn't working for me. I called producer Jim Brooks down and showed it to him. He came back, and I'm not exaggerating, it was maybe a half hour later, with new pages. He showed them to me and the scene worked.

A real producer to me is a man who can do that. Sheldon Leonard had that objectivity. Garry Marshall could do that. Norman Lear could do that. But there just aren't enough show runners working today who have the talent or the tenacity to run a show the way in my mind it should be run. I've mentioned four producers who could handle the job, but I could mention eighty-two others who would just look at a bad scene and say, "Fine. Let's move on."

Producer Tom Anderson on *The Jeff Foxworthy Show* seemed to be a graduate from the school of "fine." When I directed that series during the mid-1990s, I spent most of my time being cranky on the set. I'm not proud of it. I wish that I could have been a little more patient with the writers, or a little more diplomatic with the producer. But the truth was that the material was inferior, the actor was inexperienced, and I let them know about it. Maybe I should have kept my mouth shut and just tried to stage the show to the best of my ability. I simply couldn't do it, and it ended up costing me my job.

As far as producers went, Tom Anderson was a nice guy and a lot of fun, but he simply didn't have any idea how to run a television series. I don't think he was prepared. Frankly, I don't think this guy could lead a parade, much less a network sitcom. One day I finally couldn't take it any more and I blew up at him. It wasn't the first time that I had blown up at a producer and I'm sure it won't be the last. As it turned out, Tom was not the kind of producer who could forgive and forget. He hadn't learned how to do that either. He refused to return any of my phone calls, and that was that. I was out of another job. The irony was that I wasn't as disappointed as I thought I should be.

During the 1990s loss seemed to permeate my personal and professional life. I not only broke up with *Murphy Brown*, but also *Coach, The Jeff Foxworthy Show,* and my third wife. But what I realized, more than suffering from a sense of loss, was that somewhere along in my career I had stopped having fun. *The Andy Griffith Show* had been fun. Directing *M*A*S*H* had been fun. Even directing episodes of *Murphy Brown* had been fun. But during *Coach* the fun stopped.

Was it time for me to get out? Some of my friends suggested it. Many of them were starting to retire, and it wouldn't have been a surprise if I did the same. What surprised people was that I kept working. I continued to stick with it, despite the ups and downs. I used to attribute my stick-to-itiveness to the fact that I could still have fun. But the party appeared to be over for me. What would my reasoning be now? The pay checks were still coming, but after a while even they didn't look as enticing as they once had.

After more than four decades of plotting out and eagerly anticipating the start of every television season, a sneaking sense of dread had crept into my mind. The more time I spent in Montana, the more I was slowly coming to the realization that perhaps directing didn't fit into my lifestyle anymore. I used to joke that I would die in a rehearsal hall and the cast wouldn't know it for three or four days because they would just keep right on rehearsing. Then somebody would say, "Maybe we should get a new director in here. This guy is starting to smell." That's always the way I thought I would end up. But now, I'm not as certain as I once was. Perhaps I am ready for retirement after all.

When I sit at the monthly dinners with Yarmy's Army, I often look around the tables at the other participants. One of the things that always strikes me is that despite how talented many of the men are, most of them don't get enough work. Ageism is rampant in the entertainment business, and it seems to have attacked so many of my friends. They want to work. They have the ability to work. But the jobs are being handed out by the young to the young. Nobody forces you to retire. They just don't audition you anymore. They simply don't hire you anymore. They just don't call you anymore. And suddenly it looked like the phone had stopped ringing for me as well.

10.

Coming Out of My So-Called Retirement

Something unexpected happened today.

I started writing this book three months ago in Montana and at the time I was beginning to prepare myself both mentally and physically for retirement. I knew it wasn't going to be easy, but I felt it was inevitable. It was simply something that I had to deal with the best way I could. Writing this book helped me keep my mind off the fact that the summer would usually be the time when I would be lining up my directing jobs for the fall. Only this year, I knew, there would be no directing jobs to look forward to.

Then today the phone rang. I anxiously raced to pick it up, as I always have done out of habit, thinking it's either very good news or very bad. And much to my surprise, the call was my agent with an offer to direct a new NBC sitcom called *Chicago Sons* starring Jason Bateman. It was going to be a mid-season replacement for the network. I had already seen the pilot and remembered liking it. I had to make a decision right there on the spot. Here I was preparing for my professional retirement, yet I was being lured back with the promise of another job in just one phone call. It was an offer too good to resist. I told my agent that I would accept the job and hung up the phone. However, suddenly, I felt an overwhelming sense of confusion, rather than the elation that had usually followed this kind of call.

Only a year earlier, I would have been sky high if I'd gotten a phone call like that. In fact, I expected most phone calls to bring job offers and when they didn't I would be disappointed. What was so different about this call then? Things had changed. Hollywood had changed. I had changed. I had weaned myself away from television. Now I felt like the drug addict suddenly slipping back into his old habit again, finding the temptation too much to pass up. I literally could feel the rush of adrenaline pumping through my body as I thought about the possibility of returning to work on a soundstage. I remembered the perks that come with the job, the questions that only I could answer, and the rehearsals the cast and I would struggle through together. Just the mere thought of working again filled me with excitement.

Although in the past my whole life was directing, now there was so much more to my life. There was so much more to me. I was not just Alan Rafkin the director anymore. I had my house and friends in Montana. I had my poker games, my tennis matches, and my dinner parties. I had my daughter Dru living in New York City on her own. I had my other daughter Leigh living in San Francisco with her husband, Todd, and my grandson, Kyle. And I had started dating again. I knew I never wanted to get married again. But I also knew that I didn't want to end up eighty years old and alone either.

I finally had the kind of life that I had dreamed of and there was the darn telephone trying to pull me back into show business. I tried to quickly put things in perspective. Would it be fun to work again? Yes. Did I want to shoot an entire sitcom season? No. Would it be possible to shoot just a few episodes a year, just to keep my hand in directing? Maybe. I'd have to wait and see. Was it nice to be asked again to direct a sitcom? Absolutely. Directing was my lifeline and when it looked like I might never work again, it was like facing death. But now I was given a reprieve in the eleventh hour.

After three divorces, I told myself that maybe I was just one of those men who wasn't meant to be in a committed relationship for any great length of time. Although I had married each of my wives for very different reasons, all three relationships had fallen apart and caused pain for everyone involved. Marriage looked like it was more trouble than it was worth. Aside from giving me two fantastic daughters, what other joy did the unions bring? I tried to tell myself that it was okay to fail at relationships. I tried to convince myself that I didn't need to share my life with another woman. I even tried to picture my life without another woman, but that didn't seem right either.

A lot of the women I meet lately are very desperate and want to rush into a relationship without even getting to know me. I was with a woman at a party recently and someone mentioned a vacation cruise that they had taken recently. The woman I was with leaned over and whispered in my ear, "Someday we'll go on a cruise." I hardly knew the woman. Nobody needs that kind of aggravation.

Some of the women I meet and go out with are younger than I, and that's hard, too. If I meet a woman in her fifties, I wonder how many years I'll have to give to her. I wonder what I will be like when she is sixty and I am seventy-eight. I wonder what the life of a seventy-eight-year-old man looks like? Is it rich and fun, or difficult and depressing? What will I feel like? What will I look like? I don't know many people that age so it scares me a lot. Inside, I still feel thirty-five years old mentally and physically. When I think about the fact that I am really sixty-eight, I want to shout out, "Oh, no. You've got it all wrong." I'm simply not that old in my mind.

I'm trying to be realistic about relationships for the first time in my life. Since I was very young I always wanted to be married because I thought that was what you did when you reached a certain age. My grandparents got married, my parents got married, and I thought that I was supposed to get married. I never really thought about *not* doing it, because marriage was as basic to me as heading off to work in the morning and going to sleep at night. But I tied the knot three times and never got it right. Maybe I wanted it to work out so badly, that I ended up ruining it each time. Now I realize that maybe it is better to be with a woman, and enjoy my time with a woman, and *not* be married. Life is better than it has ever been, and I don't want to do anything to disrupt the peace and tranquility. I'm enjoying myself far too much to rock the boat.

So, I directed the episode of *Chicago Sons* and had a great time doing it. I felt the same rush. I felt the same thrill. I felt the same high. But something was missing. Something just wasn't the same. I realized that in my mind I had already retired and that's why going back felt more uncomfortable than familiar. Although I would still like to direct off and on, the desire to continue at a full-time pace has finally left me.

We had an opening night party for *Chicago Sons* at a restaurant in Santa Monica where we all watched the show on the air together. After enjoying the party, I got into my car at around 10:30 P.M. to head home. I knew that my mother hadn't been feeling well, so on the way I decided to stop by her apartment to check in. I arrived to find that my mother was dying. Her caregiver tried to comfort me. "Why don't you hold your mother's hand?" she said.

"Hold her hand?" I asked. "But I can't do that. She doesn't like me."

I remembered how she used to bristle from my hugs as a child.

"It's okay now," said the caregiver. "Go ahead and hold her hand."

So I held my mother's hand. As it lay in mine, her hand was sore and swollen from fluid but it still felt wonderful to me. I imagined that I was channeling because I started to talk to my mother about our relationship, and I think she understood. It had been contentious, but deep down we had always loved each other but just had never figured out a way to get along. I told her now she would be happy because she was going to a place where she could be with my father and her sisters and brothers again. I continued to talk and talk, telling her what fun she would have. It had never before been so easy for me to talk with my mother and it felt marvelous.

I left her apartment close to 1:30 P.M. and drove back to my apartment. Around four o'clock in the morning, I got a call from the caregiver who said that my mother had died. So it seemed that fate had taken hold of me and made me drive to her apartment that night so I could say good-bye. I felt somehow that a sense of guilt had been lifted from my shoulders. I felt very lucky to have had the chance to talk to her before she died. I felt lucky to have known her.

I can still work as hard and as long as I did twenty years ago, but Saturday morning when I woke up after shooting the episode of *Chicago Sons*, I felt a little stiffer than I used to. I needed more time to stretch out my muscles before going to my nine o'clock tennis match. My body was telling me to take it easy, and I couldn't ignore the signs.

Since starting my directing career more than four decades ago, I've directed more than eighty different TV series, many multiple times, adding up to some 800 half hours of television. It may not be in *The Guinness Book of World Records*, but it certainly is about as many episodes as anybody can do in this type of a career. I can look back at my career now with pride, rather than discomfort or inadequacy. Nostalgia has replaced my anxiety, and writing this book has been part of the cure. It has forced me to go back over my life and relive both the highs and lows of my career.

When producers look at my résumé and see that I have directed such legendary sitcoms as *The Andy Griffith Show* and *M*A*S*H*, I know immediately some think negatively, "This guy is old." They have dozens of other résumés in their piles including directors in their twenties fresh from college or graduate school whose first directing job was just a season ago on *Friends* or *Ellen*. The producers, many also in their twenties and thirties, can't imagine that someone who directed *The Andy Griffith Show* could still be alive, let alone still working as a prime-time sitcom director.

Not so long ago, my management company, Brillstein-Grey, pitched me for a job on a TV series and one of the producers asked to see my "reel." A reel is a collection of clips from a director's body of work, like a visual résumé, that is usually only asked for from beginners new to the business. My manager, Bernie Brillstein, told the producers who asked for my reel, "No. We don't have a reel for Alan, but we can send you an Emmy." Needless to say I didn't pursue the job, and they didn't come looking for me either.

In 1996, when I started to curtail my directing schedule (or Hollywood started to cut back on using me), I began to notice that making my home in Los Angeles was becoming less and less appropriate. Los Angeles is a company town like Detroit is a car town and northern California's Silicon Valley is a high-tech town. When you don't work in the entertainment business in Los Angeles, you begin to ask yourself, "What am I doing living here at all?"

I've lived through an actors' strike and a writers' strike and they were two of the most depressing times I've ever spent in Los Angeles. It was as if a pall had fallen over the entire city because everybody was out of work and nobody knew what to do with their newfound free time. Everybody was losing money, and nobody could predict when the strike was going to come to an end. Los Angeles is a town that eats, breathes, and sleeps show business. Witnessing a union strike in the town is testimony to that. And if you suddenly find yourself out of the business altogether, then there is little reason to call Hollywood your home.

That's where I found myself in January 1997. I knew that I couldn't live in Montana all year round because the winter weather would kill me, but living in my condominium on Wilshire Boulevard near Westwood the rest of the time seemed pointless. Aside from eating in a few great restaurants, there was little to keep me in Los Angeles. Both my daughters had moved away. Some of my friends had died and others had retired to other parts of the state and country. The city simply wasn't a very friendly place to outsiders, and I felt like an outsider when I wasn't working.

Everyone involved in the entertainment industry has so much emotion invested in their work that they have little energy left to do "normal" people things like make non–show business friends and play sports. It was also frustrating for me to see all of the industry energy whirling around me and not to be a part of it anymore. I wasn't reading scripts, making deals, or even going to rehearsals. I was out of the loop.

So, I decided to move to Rancho Mirage, a community two hours from Los Angeles. I chose the city because that is where my best friend, Marshall, and his wife, Judy, live. It is close enough to Hollywood so I can drive in to direct once in a while or pay a friend a visit, but far enough away so I won't be face-to-face with show business every day. To watch the industry without working in it is simply too painful for me. It makes me feel old on the outside when I don't feel old on the inside.

So far the move to Rancho Mirage has proved to be a wise one. I've noticed a correlation between the people who live in Rancho Mirage and those in Montana. Neither group appears to be out to prove anything. They are people who enjoy spending time together and appreciate conversation and companionship. Civility seems like such a simple concept, but when an angry young girl gave me the finger from a car in Los Angeles the other day, I couldn't wait to get back to Rancho Mirage.

I've only been living here a few months, but already I can feel the tension and pressure leaving my body. In the beginning I tried going back to Los Angeles once a week for my poker game, but now I've even eliminated that. I don't need it anymore. I play tennis every day here, and I've never felt so relaxed in my life. I've even given up the visits to my psychiatrist. All the therapy I need now seems to be right here in my new home in Rancho Mirage.

I always valued my role as father from the day the girls came into my life, but now I seem to luxuriate in it. I can't spend enough time with Dru and Leigh, and I enjoy just being in the same room with them. Some fathers remember the best time they ever spent with their children was when they were toddlers running around exploring their new environment. But I think the best time for me as a parent is now, when I can talk to my children as adults. The three of us are able to share our experiences, both good and bad, like relatives as well as friends, which is very special to all three of us.

One of my greatest joys is that the girls are close to each other. When they were younger they fought and squabbled, as sisters close in age often do. Dru would get Leigh in trouble. Leigh would get Dru in trouble. And Daddy would try to be the referee as best he could. But as they've gotten older, I've witnessed a metamorphosis in their relationship. Dru often spends her vacation time in San Francisco with Leigh and her family. My ex-wife Ann lives in the Bay Area as well, which also helps to bring the two sisters together. They are finding that as they march through their thirtysomething years, they have more in common instead of less. I couldn't have hoped for anything more wonderful.

Professionally both daughters are also making me proud. As of the writing of this book, Dru was thirty-two years old and the script supervisor for *Spin City*, a successful Michael J. Fox sitcom on ABC. Dru is not only considered one of the best at what she does, but she is also, in my unbiased opinion, a terrific human being. She is my older daughter, and also my dear buddy and great friend. She was the first person I ever loved unconditionally, and the first to love me back in the same way. The bond we have today is as strong as it was when we first laid eyes on each other at Cedars of Lebanon Hospital.

At the time of this book, Leigh was twenty-seven years old and married to Todd, who I think is just terrific. If we sound like a family crazy for each other we are. Leigh and Todd work in San Francisco restaurants (she as a chef, he as a sommelier and beverage manager) gathering experience in the hopes of opening their own restaurant some day. In addition to their culinary aspirations, they have to keep up with my toddler grandson Kyle, who continues to amaze me more each day.

I relish the time I spend with my grandson, especially because Leigh was around his age when her mother and I got divorced. I feel that Kyle is allowing me to share in perhaps some of the toddler moments that I might have missed with Leigh. Rather than me imparting some grandfatherly wisdom to Kyle, he is teaching me how to enjoy life again by running through a pile of leaves in the park, or darting in between furniture in his living room. It's exciting for me just to watch him learn about life.

Some days when I was directing a sitcom and we would get a note from a producer or network executive, that note might turn our entire sitcom world upside down. The actors and I would say to ourselves, "How are we going to deal with this?" or "How will we ever make this change given the amount of time we have until show night?" In television there were always setbacks; and during many years in the business, as one might expect, I learned how to deal with most problems. But what I didn't expect was that I would have a personal setback in 1996, and that it would have to do with the health of my daughter Leigh.

One day Kyle was acting like a typical rambunctious toddler and he accidentally broke his mother's eyeglasses. When Leigh went to the eye doctor to get a new pair, she needed to take an eye exam because it had been a while since her last visit. The results from the exam soon revealed the unthinkable: cancer. Leigh had a tumor growing behind one of her eyes.

Then we received more bad news. The tumor was malignant. Leigh went to several eye doctors and most said she had no choice but to lose the eye. Although Leigh remained upbeat throughout ("It's only an eye, Dad"), it was difficult to think of a twenty-seven-year-old woman losing her eye, especially when that woman was my daughter. Finally, Leigh found a doctor who suggested she try radiation in an effort to save the eye. Radiation is the kind of thing that you hope your child never ever has to go through, but when she does you have to try and be as supportive as possible while hiding the fact that you are crumbling inside.

Around the time that Leigh began her radiation, my mother passed away. Everywhere I looked I was reminded of how fragile life was. My mother had lived a long life and died of old age. That was something I could understand. But what was far more difficult for me to comprehend was the how and why behind the fact that my daughter had cancer. I couldn't help remembering several years earlier when Leigh's birth mother had contacted her and tried to initiate a relationship. I remember being afraid that my role as her adoptive father would be diminished by this new woman in her life. But Leigh said to me, "Don't worry. I already have a mommy and a daddy. This woman is something different." She showed me that adoption had nothing to do with our feelings for each other. Ann and I had changed her diapers. Ann and I had raised her. And Ann and I were her parents. During her radiation treatment, I tried to give Leigh as much love and support as I could. As I write this we are still waiting to hear the outcome of her treatment. If hope has anything to do with it, we will get the good news we want.

Part of my time away from directing is spent with my daughters, but I also spend time doing some of the things I never had time to do. Ironically, one of those things is watching television. The less television I directed, the more television I had time to watch. I was quite surprised to find that, contrary to the negative rep that television often receives in this country, there is actually some quality programming on the air. *Frasier*, I think, is exceptionally well written and well acted. I also enjoy watching *Ellen, Seinfeld,* and *Third Rock from the Sun.* Of course, I think there are a lot of mediocre shows on the air, but with the good shows come a batch of bad as well.

As I've been reflecting on my life, I've also been reflecting on television's life. I decided to write down a few lists about my personal likes and dislikes about television over the years:

The Best Sitcoms
(in no particular order)

*M*A*S*H*
The Mary Tyler Moore Show
The Dick Van Dyke Show
Frasier

The Andy Griffith Show
My World and Welcome to It
The Bob Newhart Show
It's Garry Shandling's Show

The Worst Sitcom
(in a very particular order)
The Nanny

Actors Who Never Should Have Been Cast in a Sitcom

Ann Sheridan (*Pistols 'n' Petticoats*)
Jean Arthur (*The Jean Arthur Show*)
Robert Mitchum (*A Family for Joe*)
Anthony Perkins (a pilot called *Ghost Writer*)
Richard Castellano (*The Super*)

Favorite Sitcom Actresses

Candice Bergen
Inger Stevens
Suzanne Pleshette
Shelley Fabares

Favorite Sitcom Actors

Dick Van Dyke
Bob Newhart
Tim Conway
Harvey Korman
Grant Shaud
Charles Kimbrough
Jerry Van Dyke

Most Talented Performer I Never Directed

Tracey Ullman

Actors Whose Performances Always Make Me Laugh

Tim Conway
Harvey Korman
Dom DeLuise
Jerry Van Dyke
Sam Kineson
Ron Carey
Tracey Ullman
Ellen DeGeneres

Best TV Producers

Bill D'Angelo (*Love, American Style*)
Danny Arnold (*My World and Welcome to It*)
Donzig and Peterman (*Murphy Brown*)
Tom Patchet and Jay Tarses (*The Bob Newhart Show*)
Sheldon Leonard
Norman Lear
James Brooks

TV Directors I Admire

James Burrows
John Rich
Jay Sandrich

One of the things I've noticed about television lately is that you don't see many heroes on the air anymore. When I was growing up, you would see Spencer Tracy in one or two movies a year. But you didn't know anything about his personal life. You didn't see him being interviewed on *Entertainment Tonight*. You didn't read about him in the pages of *People Magazine*. And you didn't hear about him in the gossip columns. Today our society is so obsessed with trashing its movie and television actors that there's very little room for the actors to surprise, please, and entertain us. People can more easily recite who's sleeping with whom, than the plot of their favorite TV series.

Sadly, as the role of the actor has changed in television, so has the role of the director. The job has become less important. If you walk onto any sitcom set you can see it immediately. It's the writer-producers who call the shots, pulling the strings of most of the puppet directors in the business today. When I started in show business a director on a sitcom was similar to the director on a movie set. He called the shots and ruled the set like a true leader. Today, that power has shifted, and the director is more like the British monarch. A director has the title, but little power to make decisions or change the way the empire is run.

I don't know if a lot of directors feel the way I do, because oddly enough I don't know a lot of other television directors. I'm friendly with director Jay Sandrich, who has worked in the business for years, and a few others who are members of Yarmy's Army. But most of my friends in the entertainment business are actors because those are the people I worked with on a daily basis. Many of my closest friends are older character actors, whom I've known over the years on a variety of series, rather than the more famous sitcom stars whom I worked with for a season or two and then never saw in person again.

I still admire actors as much as I did in the beginning. My secret fantasy is to go out of this business as an actor. I think I've probably been a closet actor all of my life but been too busy directing to admit it. I remember in the beginning I really entered this business with the intention of becoming an actor after paying my dues as a stand-up comedian. But early on I saw how painful the life of an actor could be, and that frightened me. I remember worrying that I might suddenly wake up and be seventy years old and have little to show for it. I didn't want to end up a bitter man, as I had seen my father become. I wanted to be proud of my work when all was said and done. Acting didn't seem to offer the security that directing could provide.

I have actor friends in their seventies now who have little financial security to show for their many years of hard work in television. A seventy-year-old who has to worry about how he's going to pay the rent is a sad picture. The idea that I have some money takes the pressure and edge off my life. Whether I retire or not ultimately does not have to be decided on the basis of money. So now it's up to me. When is the right time to call it quits? When is the appropriate time to throw in the towel? When is it time to say enough is enough? I continue to ask myself these questions.

I've finally decided that I can't kid myself anymore. Retirement is a state of mind that I simply don't subscribe to. If I was lying in a hospital bed and an agent offered me a job I just might take it. My directing habit is so ingrained that all it would take is one good phone call to get me back on the set. If my agent called with a script that was really exciting or starred an actor I wanted to work with, I would sign on in a heartbeat. But to keep directing for the sake of directing is not my way anymore. Retirement, though, seems to be too much of an all encompassing word. If I could direct just a few shows every year for the rest of my life, that would be pretty cool.

I know I'm aging, but somehow it doesn't frighten me anymore. I love being the age I am because inside my energy feels at an all-time high. I'd be a liar if I said that I didn't think about the reality that I'm on the down side of life. Reading the obituaries is like browsing through a phone book full of friends. But I'm thankful for every day that I have to spend with my family and friends. Every day I try to make the best of my life and try to bring happiness to myself and the people around me. Is there really any other way to live a full life?

For the first time in my life I finally have a life outside of show business, whether I'm playing with my grandson, visiting my daughters, or just sitting in a chair and reading a book. Life is good no matter how I look at it. I read a lot now. I never was a voracious reader because during my working life there were always at least twenty to twenty-five weeks when there was a script to read or work on. So on the weekends when I was away from the set reading was not something I cared to do. Today I finally have the time, and I'm finding more and more that I love to read. I love biographies, autobiographies, fiction, nonfiction, stories about women, and books on a range of different subjects. For so long my entertainment was limited to stories about Hollywood; now I find myself wanting to hear about the rest of the world.

Most of my life I dreamed of having a life that was different from my parents. I wanted to create a strong and close-knit family and to build a career for myself that was more satisfying than my father's had been for him. I don't think it was an accident that throughout my life I was always admiring other people's families and taking notes on how to build my own. Whether it was the Billera family back in Pennsylvania or the family of circus performers that I directed for the Ringling Brothers television special, I was always looking to surround myself with a family. I knew that when a family clicked together, there was no safer or more creative place to be on the earth.

I was very fortunate in my life that I not only was able to experience a family in the traditional sense through my two daughters, but also in the professional arena through my friends and colleagues on the sitcoms I directed. Whether it was the cast of *The Andy Griffith Show*, *M*A*S*H*, *One Day at a Time*, or *Murphy Brown*, we were in it together and did the best we could. We tried to be supportive and helpful as well as avuncular and critical all for the good of the series and the advancement of our careers. Sometimes it worked and sometimes it didn't, but I think that's pretty typical of most families you'll meet. There are no guarantees. You can only hope that the good days outnumber the bad days.

◢ ◢ ◢ ◢ ◢

Paddy Chayefsky once said that television is a god-damned amusement park—television is a circus, a carnival, a traveling troupe of acrobats, storytellers, dancers, singers, jugglers, sideshow freaks, lion tamers, and football players. We're in the boredom-killing business.

For more than four decades I have been in the boredom-killing business, and my job has been to take all of the crazy and wonderful people under the big top and help them make sense. The sitcom director is the ringmaster and that's who I was. And boy did I enjoy it. I loved the parking space with my name on it. I liked how the studio gate guard waved me in. I liked walking onto the soundstage and having everyone look toward me to solve problems. I liked the actors, producers, and crew who worked with me to make a show that would go on the air and be watched by millions across America. I liked my job and even though I always felt envy for the actors, I wouldn't have traded my job for any other in the world.

One of the highest compliments I ever received was when I was directing an episode of *Sanford and Son* in Hawaii and producer Sheldon Leonard was on the set. I had hired him as an actor to play a cameo as his typical Brooklyn tough guy. Sheldon was so used to being a producer when he watched me direct, that I think being an actor on my set gave him a different perspective on what I did and how I did it.

One day we were shooting on board a ship and Sheldon walked over to me and said, "You're very good, Alan. You know that? You're very economical with your camera. You're very good." We had been working together on sitcoms for years and that was the first time he had ever told me something like that. It was nice to hear such a compliment. Many of the people in Hollywood are too busy focusing on their own careers to stop and take the time to compliment others. Sheldon made the time, and I'll never forget it.

There came a time, when the pride I had in my own work waned and I started to question my commitment. During my last season with *Coach* I started to get tired. One night I was driving home late over Malibu Canyon Road when a policeman pulled me over. He said I was going seventy miles per hour and it looked like I had fallen asleep with my foot on the gas pedal. He didn't give me a ticket, but simply a warning telling me to wake up and be more careful. The experience scared me because I knew very well that driving seventy miles per hour over Malibu Canyon Road was difficult to do without killing yourself.

When I later mentioned the incident to my daughters, I said, "Do you ever get the feeling that you are running in so many different directions that one night you'll just fall asleep at the wheel?" I was feeling run-down, and my daughters sensed it too. Dru and Leigh called my business manager and friend Marshall and told him that I needed a driver to take me home on show nights because I was too exhausted to drive myself. So from that point forward, on Friday nights after we finished *Coach* I would get into a limousine and be taken home. It was nice because I could simply sit back and run over the night's show in my mind without having to pay attention to the road signs. I remember one night I got into the car and the driver said, "Well, Mr. Rafkin, the cash register has rung again." Even the limo driver knew that my work had become just a paycheck to me.

The soundstage had been my home base. My turf. My domain. It was where I experienced some of my happiest, saddest, and proudest moments. I achieved victories as well as disappointments. It was my world and now I had to move over. How do you slow down? How do you say good-bye? I think I can finally say I am no longer a directing addict. The value of my existence is no longer determined by which sit-com I am directing this week, but I am a director and I always will be one, whether or not I am standing on a dark soundstage. I can be thousands of miles away in Montana sitting on a lake in a speed boat and someone will ask me what I do and I will say without a moment's hesitation, "I am a director." That's the way it has always been and that's the way it will remain.

The only predictable thing about the television business is its unpredictability. Most careers teeter like a seesaw—one minute everyone loves you and next you're treated like a leper. Since I started this book I got offers to direct two episodes of *Veronica's Closet* and two of *Suddenly Susan*. I enjoyed doing them and everyone seemed to be pleased with my work. There's talk of more next season. We'll see. I also will be directing a pilot for the Henson Company. The activity is wonderful. My ego hasn't felt this good since I was mistaken for Cesar Romero . . . of course, that person was selling pencils in a tin cup . . . so maybe that doesn't count.

I'm not sure what the future will bring. But one thing I'm sure of— at this point in my life—I am a full-time grandfather and a part-time director. I will never again allow myself to get caught up in that frenzy of needing work to be happy. It's taken me sixty-seven years to figure out that there really are more important things than sitting in a control room watching my credit flash by.

I'm sitting in my den in Montana. It's seven-thirty in the morning and the sun is coming up over the lake. It looks like a Hollywood special effect. It's bright red and casting a brilliant red glow on the very still Flathead Lake. I can't help thinking what a pretty place I live in and what a wonderful career I have had. In fact, after reading this over, I had a better life than I originally thought I had. What a nice surprise.

Appendix

Index

Alan Rafkin: *A Directing Résumé*

The 1960s

77 Sunset Strip
The Andy Griffith Show
Bewitched
The Cara Williams Show
The Donna Reed Show
The Doris Day Show
The Farmer's Daughter
Get Smart
The Good Guys
I Dream of Jeannie
Laughs for Sale

Make Room for Daddy
Many Happy Returns
Mr. Terrific
My Favorite Martian
The Patty Duke Show
Pistols 'n' Petticoats
Run Buddy Run
That Girl
Valentine's Day
The Verdict Is Yours

The 1970s

Alice
Another April
Arnie
Blansky's Beauties
The Bob Newhart Show
Bridget Loves Bernie
Busting Loose
The Cop and the Kid
The Courtship of Eddie's Father
The Girl with Something Extra

The Governor and J. J.
Hanging In
Here We Go Again
Laverne & Shirley
Legs
Let's Switch
Lotsa Luck
Love, American Style
The Love Boat
The Mary Tyler Moore Show

M*A*S*H
Me and the Chimp
The Nancy Walker Show
Nanny and the Professor
The New Dick Van Dyke Show
The Odd Couple
One Day at a Time
The Partridge Family
Paul Sand in Friends and Lovers
Rhoda

Room 222
Sanford and Son
Temperatures Rising
That's My Mama
The Tim Conway Show
Viva Valdez
Wait till Your Father Gets Home
What's Happening
A Year at the Top

The 1980s

Charles in Charge
Charlie & Co.
Chicken Soup
First Impressions
Glitter
Harry's Battles
It's Garry Shandling's Show

Living in Paradise
Murphy Brown
Puppetman
Sam
She's the Sheriff
We Got It Made

The 1990s

Chicago Sons
Coach
A Family for Joe
The Ghost Writer
Hope and Gloria

The Jeff Foxworthy Show
Veronica's Closet
Suddenly Susan
Friends

Index